TRANSACTIONS OF THE

AMERICAN PHILOSOPHICAL SOCIETY

HELD AT PHILADELPHIA

FOR PROMOTING USEFUL KNOWLEDGE

VOLUME 72, PART 3

The Famine Plot Persuasion In Eighteenth-Century France

STEVEN L. KAPLAN

PROFESSOR OF HISTORY, CORNELL UNIVERSITY

THE AMERICAN PHILOSOPHICAL SOCIETY

INDEPENDENCE SQUARE: PHILADELPHIA

1982

Library of Congress Catalog
Card Number 81-71032
International Standard Book Number 0-87169-723-8
US ISSN 0065-9746

FOR SIS, MORGAN AND ASHLEY VARNER

WITH AFFECTION

CONTENTS

Introduction*

The French Revolution seethed with rumors of plots instigated by aristocrats, brigands, priests, merchants, generals, ultras, citras, mutinous workers, the queen, Pitt, and so forth. Many of them had to do with the food supply, especially with grain, from which the vast majority of Frenchmen derived most of their nourishment. These were called "famine plots," by which was meant a secret machination to starve the people in order to achieve certain ends. In the feverish months before the meeting of the Estates-General, rumors that the princes were seeking to cause famine in order to force Necker's resignation competed with others that named Necker "as the leading hoarder with the king's approval." A pamphlet circulated in the provinces denouncing an aristocratic plot aimed at preventing the convocation of the Estates-General by "introducing famine into France, causing part of the people to perish from hunger and the other part to revolt against their king." Necker's dismissal in July was perceived as part of a famine plot. One of the leading candidates for his succession, Foulon, was massacred by an avenging crowd on the grounds that he had masterminded the plot to starve the people. The famine plot was one of the leitmotifs of the Great Fear. Later in the Revolution, Lafayette, the minister Delessart, ex-king Louis Capet, and the Hébertists were all accused of plotting famine as a means to retain or usurp power.[1]

The famine plot persuasion received its most striking expression in the Revolution and there is a strong temptation to impute its paternity to the revolutionaries. But, like many attitudes and practices associated with the Revolution, the famine plot persuasion was a way of making sense of the

---

* I would like to thank the following individuals for their trenchant criticism and helpful suggestions: R. Chartier, C. C. Gillispie, D. Greenwood, S. Idzerda, Mary Ann Quinn, the members of the Early Modern European Seminar of the History Department of the Johns Hopkins University, and the members of the European History Faculty Colloquium of Cornell University.

[1] G. Rudé, *The Crowd in the French Revolution* (New York, 1969), pp. 46, 68; Sentence du Châtelet d'Orléans, FF 47, Archives communales in Archives départementales (hereafter AD) Loiret; G. Lefebvre, *La Grande Peur de 1789* (Paris, 1970), pp. 33, 34; C.-L. Chassin, *Les Elections et les cahiers de Paris en 1789* (Paris, 1889), 3: 625, 627, 634; M. du Camp, *Paris, ses organes, ses fonctions, et sa vie dans la seconde moitié du XIXe siècle* (Paris, 1869–1875), 2: 25–26; J.-C. Colfavru, "La Question des subsistances en 1789," *La Révolution française*, 5 (July–December 1883): 503; Collot d'Herbois to maire de Paris, 26 August 1793, 4 AZ 21, Archives du Département de la Seine et de la Ville de Paris (hereafter Arch. Seine-Paris); G. Schelle, ed., *Oeuvres de Turgot* (Paris, 1913–1923), 2: 46 (introd.); Mortimer-Ternaux, *Histoire de la Terreur* (Paris, 1866), 5: 175.

See also Gouverneur Morris's second-hand report of a street harangue in Paris in October 1789: "Messieurs, nous manquons du Pain, et voici la Raison. Il n'y a que trois jours que le Roi a eu ce Veto suspensif et déja les Aristocrats [sic] ont acheté des Suspensions et envoyé les Grains hors du Royaume." Gouverneur Morris, *A Diary of the French Revolution*, ed. by B. C. Davenport (Boston, 1939), 1: 244.

1

world that was deeply rooted in the collective consciousness and the material, moral and political environment of the old regime. During each of the major subsistence crises of the eighteenth century, a considerable number of Frenchmen believed that they were victims of a terrible conspiracy. The actors, modes of expression, and contents of each episode bear a striking resemblance to each other. It is as if Frenchmen were somehow constrained to see the world this way. The repetition of the same pattern of perception and evaluation in each crisis experience suggests that the famine plot persuasion was built into the structure of the collective mentality.

The famine plot persuasion was triggered by a serious and protracted disruption of the normal grain and bread supply. Consumers found reasons to question the authenticity of the dearth. They uncovered signs that the harvest was not as bad as announced, that unusual and illegal acts were occurring in the grain trade, that the government was not performing as it was supposed to, and so on. As subsistence anxiety deepened, the picture seemed to become clearer. The conviction grew that the crisis had been contrived, that there was a criminal conspiracy afoot against the people, that popular suffering was needless, and that the plotters somehow had to be resisted.

The villains were virtually interchangeable from crisis to crisis. They included men of power (ministers, *grands commis*, magistrates, and so forth), of great means (for example, financiers, tax farmers, bankers, military contractors), and members of the entourages of several of the key leaders (mistresses and relatives). Without these highly-placed persons, the plot would have been inconceivable, for it was too difficult and dangerous to launch without extraordinary protection. Other participants were recruited from more modest ranks, but they possessed skills or occupied positions crucial to the success of the conspiracy, such as merchants and brokers, millers, bakers, transporters, local officials.

The plotters were discovered mainly because their enterprise was too big to conceal. But they were also guilty of lapses, both of a personal and managerial sort. They were betrayed by their vices or by their avidity, by their inexperience or by their lack of effective control over subordinates. Their "covers"—companies or banks or certain kinds of legislation—proved to be transparent. The suspicions and accusations against them sounded a refrain that was repeated from dearth to dearth. Contemporaries denounced secret caches, illicit exports, sham imports, clandestine buying in the interior, the sale of spoiled grain, the destruction of good merchandise, price manipulation, prohibition against free marketing, the requisition of transport, the organization of spurious relief campaigns, the broadcasting of misleading news, and so on.

The famine plot persuasion was not peculiar to any one socioeconomic or cultural group. It recruited its adherents widely. Among those who subscribed to it were artisans, journeymen, *ouvrières*, day workers, peasants, soldiers, lawyers, clerks, grain dealers, magistrates, police officials, high-ranking administrators, and princes of the blood. The evidence for the existence of the persuasion comes from many different sources: the journals or letters of patrician or bourgeois observers; administrative correspondence on all levels and from many parts of the realm; parlementary papers; wall-posters, handbills, and brochures; and police reports of rumors given wide currency, of illegal public "assemblies," and of conversations and pro-nouncements in the marketplaces, taverns, churches, gardens, and streets. It is wrong to imagine that police agents related only what the government wanted to hear or what they themselves "planted," or that reports of the famine plot were isolated expressions of aberrant thinking. Many of the reports are poignantly naive portraits of the popular milieux while others bespeak a sophisticated appreciation of the portent of the information gath-ered. The decisive fact is that the reports emanate from several different sources and that they converge on the same themes. The fact that the government took the famine plot persuasion very seriously and ulcerated over it time and again suggests that it was not a marginal matter.[2]

Finally, it is important to emphasize that the famine plot persuasion was not a monolithic belief system. It had such wide sway precisely because it did not demand adherence to a doctrine or to the full sweep of suspicions and charges. It mobilized a broad range of persons who were anxious in one way or another and who perceived some sign or other that pointed to a horrible truth. Though they had different backgrounds and different motives and ambitions, nevertheless they reacted in a startlingly simi-lar way.

Let us note in passing that many historians believed and some still believe that there were real famine plots, that for various reasons the government, directly or indirectly, resorted to this dreadful maneuver in the eighteenth century.[3] Late in the nineteenth century a number of revisionist historians labored to disprove these claims. They contended that the idea of a famine plot was a legend and they used the word "legend" in a highly pejorative sense.[4] I am much less inclined to reject out of hand the possibility that

---

[2] On many occasions the police succeeded in shaping public opinion, but not during the dearths. On the methods and triumphs of the police, see Mercier's hyperbolic tribute to Parisian espionage and Lenoir's more sober recognition of its possibilities. L.-S. Mercier, *Tableau de Paris* (Amsterdam, 1782), 1: 162–63 and papiers de Lenoir, Bibliothèque municipale d'Orléans, MS. 1422 and 1423.

[3] See, for example, P. S. Laurentie, *Histoire de France* (Paris, 1845), 8: 266; G. de Molinari, article "Céréales," in Coquelin and Guillaumin, eds., *Dictionnaire de l'économie politique* (Paris, 1873), 1: 305; A. Cochut, "Le Pain à Paris," *Revue des deux mondes*, 4 (15 August 1863): 986–989; M. du Camp, *Paris*, 2: 29, 32; Mauguin, *Etudes historiques sur l'administration de l'agriculture en France* (Paris, 1876–1877), 1: pp. 326–330, 340–341; F. Rocquain, "Le Parti des philosophes," *Séances et travaux de l'Académie des sciences morales et politiques*, 14 (1880): 102–146; E. Bonnemère, *Histoire des paysans* (Paris, 1846), 2: 160–161; and most recently G. Walter, *Histoire des paysans* (Paris, 1963), p. 308.

[4] G. Bord, *Histoire du blé en France. Le Pacte de famine, histoire, légende* (Paris, 1887); L. Biollay, *Etudes économiques sur le XVIIIe siècle. Le Pacte de famine; l'administration du commerce* (Paris, 1885); G. Afanasiev, "Le Pacte de famine," *Séances et travaux de l'Académie des sciences morales et politiques*, 34 (1890): 569–593, 740–769; L. Cahen, "Le Pacte de famine et les spéculations sur les blés," *Revue Historique*, 152 (May-June 1926): 32–43 and "Le Prétendu pacte de famine. Quelques précisions nouvelles," *Revue historique*, 176 (September-October 1935): 173–216; G. Schelle, "Turgot et le pacte de famine," *Séances et travaux et l'Académie des sciences morales et politiques*, 74 (1910): 189–217.

famine plots on some scale really operated.[5] But it seems to me that the question that preoccupied the revisionist historians—whether the plots existed or not—is less interesting than the *belief in their existence*. Over time a belief acquires legendary status in a different sense: legend as the transmission of moral verities. In this perspective the famine plot is a legend not to impugn but first to document and then to ponder. We shall examine the conditions of production that generated the belief and gave it a structural character. In addition, we shall attempt to provide a context in which it can be read across the eighteenth century.

---

[5] I will suggest in what follows that the plot accusations may have been well-founded in some instances and to some degree. But I want to emphasize that in this essay I am concerned with the verisimilitude of the charges rather than with their veracity. To explore the latter would require a major study of the structures, relations, and practices of the world of victualing and its connections with public administration at all levels. I am not certain that the material for such an undertaking exists. Even if it did, one would have serious difficulty in constituting truly convincing proof (and probably in establishing evidentiary criteria). In any event, one would have to resist the mighty temptation to make the reification of the belief itself into the first article of the bill of indictment for conspiracy.

I. The Dearth of 1725-1726

Suspicions of heinous plots and maneuvers were rife during the dearth that struck the Paris region as well as Normandy and certain other areas north of the Loire in 1725-1726. Although the 1724 crop had been mediocre and the real yield of the 1725 harvest drastically diminished as a result of too much rain, contemporaries insisted that supplies were more than ample to meet provisioning needs.[6] The dearth was said to be "phony," an artificial shortage engineered to drive up prices and sustain them at levels that would assure windfall profits to a cabal of speculators. Narbonne, a police commissaire in Versailles, reported in vague but portentous terms that "emissaries" had been dispatched in the late spring of 1725 to all the farms in the vast Parisian supply zone to buy up the remaining "old" grain and grain futures at prices well above current schedules.[7] Some of this grain was known to be stored in convents, monasteries, and hospitals under the "cover" of regular institutional supply.[8] It was widely believed, according to police reports of the state of opinion in the capital, that "there are secret orders emanating from the Court that enjoin all grain merchants and *fermiers* as far away as 20, 30 and 50 leagues not to ship any grain to Paris until further notice." Similarly, millers were allegedly instructed to grind only "authorized" grain.[9] The relief measures taken by the government were denounced as a cruel cover-up. The "English" flour and "Barbary" wheat were said to be nothing other than domestic merchandise "rebaptized" in order to increase their price.[10]

---

[6] On the relative "sterility" of the 1724 harvest, see Anon., "Mémoire sur les moyens de procurer des bleds pour la subsistance de la Ville de Paris," ca. November 1725, manuscrits de la Bastille 10271, Bibliothèque de l'Arsenal (hereafter MS. Bast.) and MS. fr. 21651, fol. 285, Bibliothèque nationale (hereafter BN). On the incessant rainfall, see *Mémoires secrets de Duclos*, A. Pettitot and Monmerque, eds., *Collection des mémoires relatifs à l'histoire de France* (Paris, 1829), 77: 31, 41. Official assessments of the 1725 harvest differed sharply. For the view that it was "universally abundant, four times the harvests since 1719," see 25 September 1725, MS. Bast. 10270. For a more nuanced and pessimistic evaluation, stressing the poor quality of the crop and the resultant low yield in flour and bread, see Couet de Montbayeux to Procurator-General of Paris Parlement (hereafter PG), 9 October 1725, MS. Bast. 10270, pièces 211, 214. On the "real" abundance, see police opinion reports, Fall 1725, MS. Bast. 10277; E. J. F. Barbier, *Chronique de la régence et du règne de Louis XV (1718-63), ou Journal de Barbier* (Paris, 1858), 1: 398 (July 1725); M. Marais, *Journal et mémoires sur la régence et le règne de Louis XV (1715-1737)*, ed. by M. de Lescure (Paris, 1863-1868), 3: 211 (July 1725).

[7] P. de Narbonne, *Journal des règnes de Louis XIV et Louis XV de l'année 1701 à l'année 1744*, ed. by J. A. LeRoi (Versailles, 1866), p. 144.

[8] Anon., "Histoire de ce qui s'est passé au sujet des bleds en 1725," Recueil Fevret, MS. 3308, Arsenal. See also *Journal de Barbier* (ed. 1858), 1: 429-430 (June 1726).

[9] Gazetins de police, 8, 28 September, 15 November 1725, MS. Bast. 10155, fols. 78-79, 136. See also *Journal de Barbier* (ed. 1858), 1: 402 (August 1725) and Marais, *Journal*, 3: 215 (August 1725).

[10] Gazetins de police, 26 September 1725, MS. Bast. 10155, fol. 70.

"They are gambling with the fate of Paris and perhaps of France in this secret game," lamented the lawyer Marais.[11] For his colleague Barbier there was no doubt about who "they" were: "this dearth comes from the [royal] court." He discerned unmistakable signs of what he called a "manège" on subsistence, the very same metaphor of manipulation that St.-Simon used to describe dubious grain speculations during the subsistence crises of 1709, 1725, and 1740.[12] This was the theme of conversations in meeting places all over the capital, according to police reports. People questioned the motives and conduct of the authorities with growing "impertinence and violence."[13] "Everyone agrees that there is underhandedness [du sousterain] and venality [de l'interest] in this affair," wrote one police agent.[14] A grain and flour measurer in the Halles, as close as anyone to grassroots provisioning affairs, openly denounced the dearth as a "secret operation" of the ministry.[15] At the Marché-neuf consumers debated how much the government was reaping from its maneuvers.[16] The government has taken over the grain business, claimed a former Swiss guard, "in order to pay the king's debts."[17]

Another police agent recorded a similar point of view in an exchange of ideas in a café:

They [the king's advisers] realized that the money they took in from grain maneuvers was the surest money, for the people could not do without bread . . . [and] that was worth more than the fiftieth tax and the coronation tax [highly unpopular impositions levied in 1724–1725.][18]

"The king or his ministers," according to others, "resolved to draw 35 to 40 millions in cash from grain and flour . . . because they could not raise this sum any other way."[19] One police agent, as if to reassure himself and his superiors, maintained that only "the evil-intentioned" traded in these terrible charges.[20] But one of his colleagues insisted pointedly that "big and little and from all estates and conditions, everyone speaks this language."[21] Eager to deflect blame for rising prices from themselves, the bakers seconded

---

[11] Marais, *Journal*, 3: 215 (August 1725).

[12] *Journal de Barbier* (ed. 1858), 1: 398 (July 1725) and 402–403 (August 1725); Louis de Rouvroy, duc de Saint-Simon, *Mémoires de Saint-Simon*, ed. by A. de Boislisle (Paris, 1879–1928), 17: 200, 209–211. The word was also used in police reports (for example, "Les Messieurs Pâris qui font encore ce manège"). Fall 1725, MS. Bast. 10277.

[13] Gazetins de police, 26 September 1725, MS. Bast. 10155, fol. 68. Another agent characterized the attitude of Parisians as "a ferocious and almost desperate mistrust." 25 September 1725, MS. Bast. 10270.

[14] Gazetins de police, 26 September 1725, MS. Bast. 10155, fol. 70.

[15] 23 September 1725, ibid., fols. 64–65.

[16] 10 November 1725, ibid., fol. 125.

[17] Anon., "Mémoire de ce qui s'est passé," 9 October 1725, MS. Bast. 10033.

[18] Police report, Fall 1725, MS. Bast. 10277.

[19] Gazetins de police, 8 September 1725, MS. Bast. 10155, fols. 60–61.

[20] 15 May 1726, ibid., 10156, fol. 213.

[21] 28 September 1725, ibid., 10155, fols. 78–79. See also 30 November 1725, ibid., fol. 152 and Narbonne, *Journal*, p. 138.

the thesis that the government was responsible.[22] But Parisians betrayed
no sympathy for the bakers, whom they regarded as the covert allies of
the grain cabal. Moreover, they accused several police commissaires, who
were supposed to "contain" the bakers, of encouraging them to raise prices,
presumably upon orders from the ministry or in exchange for bribes that
the bakers paid them.[23]

All of Paris was "talking bread,"[24] but a woman from Lyon living with
two children in a furnished room near Notre-Dame rebuked them for doing
no more than talking. "Parisians should have revolted two months ago,"
she declared, ". . . at Lyon we would not have waited so long, [for] it is
very clear that the Government is hoarding grain in order to squeeze the
people dry. . . ."[25] (In fact a little more than two months before the woman
made these remarks there had been a tumultuous rising in the faubourg
St.-Antoine aimed against the bakers.[26]) At about the same time, six "officers
of the Guard" who had been in charge of the detachments assigned to
preserve order in the bread markets warned the government, in an un-
signed memorandum, that "they could no longer answer for the fidelity
of their soldiers unless you have the goodness to have the price of bread
reduced, because they are all in very great despair and they have begun
to take such liberty in what they say that we are convinced that if the least
revolt breaks out they will be the first to pillage and profit from the disorder." Nor did the soldiers entertain any doubts about the origins of the
dearth. "Everyone was persuaded" that it was the product of "the maneuvers" of Madame de Prie, mistress of the chief minister, the duc de Bourbon, in complicity with the Pâris brothers, who were financiers, military
suppliers, and ministerial counselors. The situation is volatile, the officers
admonished, "you have no time to lose."[27]

It is hard to imagine a statement of greater audacity addressed to the
royal council by minor functionaries. Though one cannot be certain that
this document was in fact written by officers of the Guard, their warnings

---

[22] Gazetins de police, 26 November 1725, MS. Bast. 10155, fol. 145. See also the report on
widow-baker Priou who "crowed against the government on the flour question." 1 December
1725, ibid., fol. 153.

[23] 16 September 1725, ibid., fols. 74–75; 26 December 1725, ibid., fol. 193; Lemoyne to Lieutenant général de police (hereafter LG), 3 November 1725, MS. Bast. 10271. In 1709, according
to Saint-Simon, "commissaires set the price at the markets peremptorily and often forced the
sellers [bakers] to raise prices against their will." Mémoires, 17: 197. There are at least two
reasons why the grain cabal might have desired to see prices rise. First, rising bread prices
reinforced the upward pressure on the mercuriale. Second, consumers would be inclined to
discharge much of their venom on the bakers—the immediate oppressor—rather than on the
far more olympian speculators.

[24] Police reports, Fall 1725, MS. Bast. 10277.

[25] Gazetins de police, 26 September 1725, MS. Bast., 10155, fol. 70.

[26] 11 July 1725, Y 12571, Archives nationales (hereafter AN).

[27] 26 September 1725, MS. Bast. 10277. The ministry referred the memorandum to the lieutenant general of police and to the commander of the Guet. Police observers reported that
Parisians regarded the quasi-military occupation of the bread-markets as a bad augury and
they resented it as an irrelevant response to their problem. See 24 November 1725, MS. Bast.
10271 and E. Raunié, ed., Recueil Clairambault-Maurepas. Chansonnier historique du 18e siècle
(Paris, 1879–1884), 5: 80.

are plausible, not only in terms of the current mood of the capital but in terms of recent experience. For the soldiers of the Guard had led the pillage of the Place Maubert bread market during the crisis of 1692 and had been a source of disorder (along with their wives) in the markets during the terrible winter of 1709.[28]

Other observers echoed the warning that Parisians were in a seditious humor. Reporting an opinion in the Luxembourg quarter, a police agent wrote that "the people are no longer satisfied with talk" and that rebellion was to be feared if bread was short in the next market.[29] In a tavern a painter named Delaunay suggested that the government organized the dearth in order to repay the huge amounts it owed the banker Samuel Bernard. If things did not quickly improve he threatened that "there would be a revolt."[30] An abbé in a conversation in the Palais-Royal passionately inveighed against the "shameful" exploitation of the people and hinted that perhaps only they could end it by taking the initiative to overthrow "Messieurs Paris, and a part of the Company of the Indies and in last resort the one-eyed bugger [Bourbon] who supports them."[31] In late September, when it appeared that bread might soon reach 10 sous the pound, five times above the price considered normal, handbills were found near city hall threatening a general rising. "We do not want to die of hunger," read the tracts, "but if we must die we are resolved to do so by forcing them [the government] to give us justice."[32]

The appearance of "abusive, threatening, and seditious" wall posters denouncing the government for causing the dearth alarmed authorities.[33] Some were crudely composed in a scrawled hand with phonetic spelling and simple language; others were boldly lettered and more sophisticated in conception. Police Inspector Bonamy found one of the first type at the corner of the Pont St.-Michel in late August. Signed the "dame ravandeuse des ale," it reviled the duc de Bourbon, "chief and protector of the Company of the Indies," for having grain sold "at three and four times more than it cost."[34] Almost a month later Commissaire Delajarie found a poster

---

[28] See Nicolas Delamare, *Traité de la police* (Paris, 1729), 2: 867 and Hérault, "La disette de pain à Paris en 1709," *Mémoires de la Société de l'Histoire de Paris*, 45 (1918): 29–31. Apparently the regular troops proved undependable in the London markets in the 1790s. C. Reith, *The Police Idea* (London, 1938), p. 106.

[29] Gazetins de police, 23 September 1725, MS. Bast. 10155, fol. 66. See also 26 December 1725, ibid., fol. 193.

[30] 27 September 1725, ibid., fol. 77.

[31] 15 November 1725, ibid., fol. 136.

[32] 24 September 1725, ibid., fol. 65.

[33] On the anxiety of officials, see duc de Bourbon to PG, 8 October 1725 and PG (draft) to Bourbon, 10 October 1725, Collection Joly de Fleury, BN (hereafter Coll. JF) 1117, fols. 210–212. At least two individuals were arrested on suspicion of having composed the poster. About the first, Sieur Mahudel, we know nothing. The second, de Poleins, blacksheep son of a prominent parlementary family from Albi, might have been a grub-street type of philosophe-social critic. Arrested in October 1725, he was released nine months later, presumably because there was insufficient evidence to convict him. Hérault to PG, 9 October 1725 and duc de Bourbon to PG, 8 October 1725, in Coll. JF 1117, fols. 208–210 and MS. Bast. 10905.

[34] 28 August 1725, MS. Bast. 10905.

of the other sort addressed to the public in general: "You are hereby informed that you will not see the price of bread go down because the ministers, Samuel Bernard and the 4 Paris [brothers] are the only grain merchants in Paris." Collective violence was the only recourse against these conspirators who had already bilked the nation of 40,000,000 livres: "We must no longer expect either succor or justice save by our own hands and our own arms, there being no other way to escape death by starvation than to pillage the rich beginning with those Buggers [the conspirators] to whom no quarter should be given." Nor were revolts always futile affairs, the poster reminded Parisians. Recent riots at Rouen and Caen had resulted in a reduction of the price of bread. Let us follow this example, exhorted the anonymous author: if we must perish, "isn't it better to die by the sword or by the bullet than by hunger like cowards?" In fact, claimed the writer, we are likely to triumph, for the soldiers of the Guard "will help and will not fire on us."[35]

In order to understand the sway and the specific character of the famine plot persuasion of 1725, we must take note of certain elements of *vraisemblance* in the charges leveled against the cabal. Even if these charges do not constitute proof by our standards, upon examination many of them do not appear incredible or groundless. They are not mere calumnies, the fruit of credulity, or the expression of lunatic fantasies. They reveal to us how and why contemporaries were led to believe in the existence of a plot. While it is clear that the ministry did not actually prohibit *fermiers* from supplying Paris,[36] there is little doubt that it did everything it could to give priority to the sale of grain directly purchased with government funds (the "king's grain," as such emergency supplies were commonly called) or commissioned by the ministry from private entrepreneurs operating theoretically at their own risk. Public provisioning was immensely expensive, and the government strained to do everything in its power to keep losses to a minimum. This was one of the reasons why "government" or king's grain

---

[35] 21 September 1725, Coll. JF 1117, fol. 223. This poster was glued to the wall with "chewed-up bread." A number of other posters were found dealing with famine plot and related issues such as onerous taxation, extortionate monetary manipulation, misery, and unemployment caused by the subsistence crisis. It is worth noting that several posters urged the parlements, as the representatives and protectors of the people, to act in their behalf against the oppressive government, a theme that was to recur in the 1740 and 1768 versions of the famine plot persuasion and to serve in a broader sense as one of the leitmotifs of parlementary politics. One poster intimated a link between grain speculation and moral dissolution, especially in sexual behavior (Bourbon's "scandalous concubinage" with de Prie). This theme reappeared toward the end of Louis' reign (the moral connection between the *parc aux cerfs* and the famine plot) and points to a larger question that merits scholarly attention: the way in which tales of sexual dissipation, transformed in many instances into a sort of political pornography, were used to undermine monarchical allegiance.

[36] There was at least one case in the fall of 1725 of a *laboureur* who complained that he had been prevented—apparently by d'Ombreval, the police chief dismissed in August—from selling his grain at the Halle. Marion to PG, 22 September 1725, Coll. JF 1117, fol. 239. It is also possible that market conditions themselves—the fear of competing against the massive royal grain machine in particular—"disgusted" *laboureurs* and deterred them from frequenting the regular grain supply markets. See, for example, the case of the boycott of Beaumont. Doubleau to Hérault, 12 October 1725, MS. Bast. 10270, pièce 237.

was usually sold at a price only a little below the going price. It was imperative to sell this grain before prices fell too much in order to assure a reasonable return and to reconstitute a purchasing fund in case more emergency supplies were needed.

The inherently complex difficulties of this sort of undertaking were aggravated by a lack of direction and coordination. Often without consulting and cross-checking, the controller-general, the lieutenant general of police, the procurator–general of the parlement, and the municipality each independently ordered public purchases or commissioned private purchases in behalf of his jurisdiction with more or less explicit guarantees against loss. The consequences of this rivalry were not only catastrophic on the buying side (prices bidded up, supply areas stripped bare) but also on the distribution side (competition for the limited means of transport available and for priority marketing).

Dodun, the controller-general, deplored "this chaos" and warned the other officials to moderate their zeal in the name of efficiency.[37] Dodun had committed the central government to the support—preferential, if not exclusive—of Samuel Bernard, who had begun an immense campaign to feed Paris at Dodun's request in November 1724.[38] Jealous prima donna as well as a crafty businessman, Bernard wanted to be the sole provider and savior of the capital and Dodun was more or less inclined to appease him. Dodun's impassioned defense of Bernard's role might have been read as proof of a plot:

As a result of his credit and his efforts, Monsieur Bernard is in a position to furnish all the quantities that we might need. He is flattered to serve as the exclusive supplier to Paris and I notice that he is hurt when we assign others to share this task with him.

The controller-general seconded Bernard's claim that the other suppliers failed to practice the proper "circumspection" in their purchases, thus driving up prices. Lacking his experience and his international network of correspondents, these other buyers conducted exchange and banking operations ineptly, to the detriment of the French economy. How could we go wrong, asked Dodun, when "a million [livres] in purchases made by M. Bernard in foreign countries does less damage to the grain price and exchange structures than 100,000 in purchases by other individuals?"[39]

The extraordinary royal protection accorded Bernard exasperated other suppliers (many of whom were professionals, long engaged in the provi-

---

[37] Controller-general (hereafter CG) to Hérault, 2 September 1725, G⁷ 35, AN.

[38] Duc de Bourbon to Bernard, 6 November 1724, G⁷ 33, AN.

[39] CG to PG, 27 January 1726, Coll. JF 1118, fols. 51–52. Cf. the complaint that the offers of assistance of a "famous Genevan merchant and banker established in Paris" had been rebuffed because Bernard exercised "the general direction of all the grain." Anon., "Histoire de ce qui s'est passé au sujet des bleds en 1725," MS. 3308, Arsenal. The Genevan was probably Barthélémy Favre. See H. Lüthy, *La Banque protestante en France de la révocation de l'édit de Nantes à la Révolution* (Paris, 1959–1961).

sioning trade), and their grumbling may have contributed to public suspicions. Marquet, commissioned by the lieutenant of police to bring in grain and flour from Languedoc, protested that he lost over 15,000 livres because of delays caused by Bernard's monopoly on shipping from Rouen to the capital.[40] Flour dealers Olivier and Delarue suffered similar prejudice for the same reasons.[41] Anomalous situations arose that were bound to raise questions and nourish rumors. Normally anyone registered for the grain trade could supply Paris, and in crisis periods such help was usually more welcome than ever. It appears, however, that in 1725 dealers without special commissions had to request permission to market their merchandise in the capital. A Pontoise merchant had to call upon an influential friend to intervene before he was allowed to unload his boatload of Dutch grain, and it is possible that there were instances when such authorization was not forthcoming.[42]

Indeed, for at least a short time in the fall of 1725 there seemed to be *too much* grain in Paris, though bread prices remained extremely high (in part because the climate of uncertainty persisted and because bad weather prevented the mills from transforming enough grain into flour).[43] In light of mounds of visible abundance, what were anxious consumers to think? Dodun harshly reproached the bakers for not buying up the merchandise that was available.[44] To oblige the bakers to absorb this government grain, it is possible that Hérault, the lieutenant general of police, momentarily asked the hinterland *laboureurs* and *fermiers* to stay off the market (though, on the other hand, we know that since his appointment the previous August Hérault had been trying to impose formal supply quotas on the habitual Paris-area suppliers in order to assure a regular supply).[45]

With the aim of dissipating suspicions by removing their visible source and of preventing spoilage of the grain that stood exposed in the uncovered ports and Halle, the police decided to store the grain in various improvised locations throughout the city.[46] Grain (mostly Bernard's) was placed in hospitals, colleges, religious communities, enclosed tennis courts, and in the

---

[40] Marquet to LG, 10 September 1726, MS. Bast. 10273.

[41] Intendant of Rouen to LG, 24 January 1726, MS. Bast. 10272. Note the incredulous tone of Delarue when he learned of the government's intention to postpone the marketing of his flour—merchandise that he presumed was desperately needed. To Hérault, 8 December 1725, MS. Bast. 10271.

[42] De Tourmont to LG, 27 October 1725, MS. Bast. 10271. On the absence of dealers on the Paris markets save those operating "for the account of the king," see CG to duc de Luxembourg, 4 August 1725, G⁷ 34, AN.

[43] On the importance of flour crises, frequently overlooked by historians, see S. L. Kaplan, *Bread, Politics and Political Economy in the Reign of Louis XV* (The Hague, 1976), 1: xvi, 310–311.

[44] CG to Prévôt des Marchands, 25 October 1725, G⁷ 34, AN. See also 9 October 1725, Coll. JF 1117, fol. 61.

[45] MS. Bast. 10270, pièces 48, 51, 53 and Coll. JF 1117, fol. 53. There was also a quota system imposed by the controller-general on the intendants of the generalities near Paris who then decided how best to raise the required amounts. See, for example, CG to Intendant of Châlons, 12 September 1725, G⁷ 35, AN.

[46] Bourlon to LG, 4 October 1725, MS. Bast. 10270, pièce 273.

public buildings of neighboring towns, such as St.-Germain.[47] These trans-
fers may have saved some grain from further deterioration, but they succeeded mainly in heightening suspicions. The police tried to move the grain
surreptitiously, but it was impossible to relocate several thousands of *muids*
discreetly.[48] Parisians were already predisposed to expect "maneuvers,"
usually at night. The theatrically conspiratorial gestures of the police served
only to confirm their worst fears: if grain was being stocked—hidden?—in
convents and other institutional buildings, it was for the purpose of maintaining high prices and public misery.

Bernard himself was fully aware of the dilemma. "If there occurs the
slightest price rise," he wrote Dodun, "it will be blamed on the wheat that
we have stored in the Invalides."[49] For all his cunning, Bernard made the
mistake of sending servants dressed in his well known livery to see how
things were going in various storage places and markets.[50] Parisians unaware of the connection between government grain and these makeshift
granaries were tempted to wonder whether the monasteries and convents
were not also engaged in hoarding, an accusation that was to gain currency
in the course of the century as the Parisian police attempted to transform
the religious communities into a permanent, emergency grain reserve
network.[51]

The fear of spoilage was another incentive for authorities to give priority
to the sale of royal grain (much of it foreign merchandise) over ordinary
hinterland supplies. Not only did this help give credibility to the charges
that regular dealers were being diverted away from the capital, but it also
added a new dimension to the plot scenario: the conspirators did not hesitate
to sell Parisians rotten goods (at exorbitant prices nevertheless!) even at the
risk of making them sick—such was their viciousness. There was an un-
derstandable a priori prejudice against foreign grain.[52] It had to travel vast
distances, often in abominable conditions. Even where there was no negligence or bad will, it was bound to deteriorate, for conservation and restoration technology was relatively primitive.[53] Commonly, when it arrived,

---

[47] PG to LG, 14 December 1725, MS. Bast. 10271; deliberations of bureau of Hôtel-Dieu, 3
May 1726, Archives de l'Assistance publique (hereafter AAP), no. 95; LG to PG, 13 February
1726, Coll. JF 1116, fol. 186; Legrand to LG, 4 May 1726, MS. Bast. 10273; Couet de Montbayeux
to PG, 24 October 1725, Coll. JF. 1116, fols. 198–199.

[48] A muid, Paris measure, contained 12 setiers, each theoretically weighing 240 livres. In
modern French volume measure, a muid is the equivalent of 18.73 hectolitres.

[49] Bernard to CG, 18 October 1725, G⁷ 34, AN.

[50] Gazetins de police, 26 September 1725, MS. Bast. 10155, fol. 74.

[51] See my "Lean Years, Fat Years: the 'Community' Granary System and the Search for
Abundance in Eighteenth-Century Paris," *French Historical Studies*, 10, (Fall, 1977): 197–230.

[52] See, for example, *Journal de Trévoux* (October 1755), 2600; Coll. JF 1120, fols. 8–9; "Mémoire
sur les grains étrangers," ca. 1726, G⁷ 1660–1665, AN.

[53] On matters of conservation, see E. Béguillet, *Traité des subsistances et des grains qui servent
à la nourriture de l'homme* (Paris, 1780), pp. 212–213, 365–366; A. A. Parmentier, *Le Parfait
boulanger, ou traité complet sur la fabrication et le commerce du pain* (Paris, 1778); Jollivet de
Vannes, "Mémoire," January 1764, O¹ 361, AN; F. Lacombe, *Le Mitron de Vaugirard, dialogues
sur le bled, la farine et le pain* (Amsterdam, 1777); Turgot, "Septième lettre sur le commerce des
grains," October 1770, in Schelle, ed., *Oeuvres de Turgot*, 3: 145. One notes with a sense of
irony that one of the leading sponsors of research into conservation technology was Pâris-

it had a bad odor (that became a bad taste) or it was overheated or humid. Moreover, sometimes this foreign grain was very different from the kind with which Parisian bakers and consumers were familiar and thus produced a loaf that they both deemed unworthy and suspect.[54] In 1725 Parisians complained bitterly of the bread of "bad quality" that they were forced to eat as a result of "the traffic of Messrs Pâris and M. Bernard."[55]

In fact the bakers admitted that their bread was occasionally bad and blamed it on the government for constraining them to purchase "rotten" or "altered" flour.[56] There is no doubt that the authorities did put pressure on the bakers to use merchandise of dubious quality, albeit not genuinely rotten and therefore dangerous. As long as it was edible, the government felt that it was a precious crisis resource (though Parisians proved time and again in the eighteenth century that it is simply not true that if people are hungry enough they will eat anything). Moreover, the government was worried about the cost of the spoilage as well as the need to utilize all possible supplies. The "états des bleds deffectueux et des farines gatez" suggest that losses were quite large in 1725-1726.[57] Officials tried to "repair" the damaged merchandise, but if they judged the quality egregiously below Parisian standards, they offered it for purchase to the institutions of public assistance (which, incidentally, were not generally inclined to absorb such goods) or to provincial consumers whose standards were a lot less lofty than those of Parisians.[58]

Duverney, one of the alleged famine plotters. 28 April 1762, 22 March 1765, Y 12611, AN; 127 AP, AN; Mareschal to editor, 30 April 1781, *Journal de Paris*, no. 120; J. Savary des Bruslons, *Dictionnaire portatif de commerce* (Copenhagen, 1761), 3: 141.

[54] In 1725-1726 the lieutenant of police distributed instruction booklets to millers and bakers showing how to use Sicilian, Levantine, and other foreign grain. 31 January 1726, MS. Bast. 10156, fol. 45 and Coll. JF, 1117, fol. 25. Two bakers were sent from Marseille to teach Parisians how to knead Mediterranean grain. 4, 24 January 1726, MS. Bast. 10149.

[55] 5, 30 November 1725, MS. Bast. 10155, fols. 116, 152. Flour quality was so bad that Hérault received personal requests from influential courtiers to arrange to supply their bakers with "good flour." See de Conflans to LG, 29 November 1725, MS. Bast. 10271 and Gourgeon to LG, October 1725, ibid. The lieutenant general of police's grain conservation specialist warned of ongoing difficulties in the summer of 1726: ". . . les bleds et farines continuent de se gatter. Il est même dangereuse que si l'on ne travaille promptement à réparer ceux même qui ne paroissent pas encore gattez, il n'en proviene des prèjudices considérables à la santé publique [sic]." Pichon to Hérault, 11 July 1726, MS. Bast. 10273.

[56] Gazetins de police, 15 November 1725 and 10, 23 March 1726, MS. Bast. 10155, fol. 38 and 10156, fols. 103, 121. Toward the end of the century Mercier gave credence to the claim that the government sometimes "forced people to eat rotten wheat," specifically in the Parisian faubourgs. *Tableau de Paris* (Amsterdam, 1783), 3: 204. In 1528 a number of London bakers preferred to go to jail rather than use the wheat and rye supplied by the government which they judged "musty and not holsam for mannes body." S. Thrupp, *A Short History of the Worshipful Company of Bakers of London* (London, 1933), p. 78.

[57] *Etat*, 11 January-26 July 1726, MS. Bast. 10273; Coll. JF 1117, fol. 165.

[58] See PG to LG, 14 December 1725, MS. Bast. 10271. Spoilage of foreign grain was not inevitable. Ironically, it was a concern for a certain kind of economy that may have been responsible for some of the deterioration. Stored grain was not as a rule sifted—a basic conservation technique—because sifting resulted in a diminution of the total amount of grain through wastage. Couet de Montbayeux to PG, 24 October 1725, Coll. JF 1117, fols. 240-243. See also the practice of the Roman emperors who "disguised" spoiled old grain with new grain in order to sell it and thereby avoid financial losses. Béguillet, *Traité des Subsistances*, pp. 321-322.

It is evident that much of the "bad" grain did indeed belong to the massive Bernard stocks. On several occasions commissaire Duplessis halted the sale of Bernard grain or flour because it produced bread with "a very bad taste."[59] Commissaire Narbonne reported that Bernard was compelled to have "a prodigious quantity" of his irretrievably rotten grain thrown in the Seine.[60] But that, too, exposed him and the ministry to the merciless double bind. On the one hand, if they had placed that merchandise in circulation, they would have been accused of the cruelest trafficking. On the other hand, few Parisians were willing to believe that it was rotten grain that Bernard jettisoned.[61] Rather, it was depicted as passable merchandise purposely discarded, despite urgent public needs, in order to prolong the scarcity and the cutthroat prices.[62]

The impression of *vraisemblance* seems even stronger when we look more closely at the roles played by the alleged conspirators. What made this crime against the people so odious, so shocking, and so menacing was that it was organized under the aegis of the most powerful man in France, the duc de Bourbon, chief minister and prince of the blood. It is hard to find anything flattering to say about him. According to most reports, he was ugly, narrow-minded, and dull. The dearth made him hateful, for, as a popular song put it, he was the ruler who "wanted to make the poor people of Paris die of hunger."[63] If we are to believe Narbonne, Bourbon's heartlessness may have had political as well as venal motives, for rumor had it that the duke believed that France was overpopulated and "that it was [therefore] necessary to cause some of the populace to perish from misery."[64] Given this bloodthirsty image, it was now easy to believe that Bourbon had

---

[59] Duplessis to PG, 13, 14, July 1726, Coll. JF 1118, fols. 174–175. See also Cleret to Hérault, 1 October 1735, MS. Bast. 10270, fols. 329–330.

[60] Narbonne, *Journal*, p. 138.

[61] Thirion, *Madame de Prie, 1689–1727* (Paris, 1905), p. 238.

[62] The tossing of grain in the local river forms one of the abiding themes of the famine plot persuasion throughout France. See, for instance, the grain that Saint-Simon reported to have been cast in the Loire by the agents of "Messieurs des finances" in 1709. *Mémoires*, 17: 197. This charge is redolent of recent "eyewitness" reports circulating in the United States "that oil company tankers have dumped thousands of gallons of oil in the desert, just to keep it off the market." *Newsweek*, 21 May 1979. One cannot reflect on recent "plot" phenomena without calling to mind the infamous Russian-American grain deal of 1972. There is considerable evidence that it was the fruit of a conspiracy. The plot involved a handful of fabulously wealthy and powerful international grain traders, officials of the United States government (some of whom had worked or were about to work for the grain merchants), jet-setting influence-peddlers, and lobbyists. The chief victims of the plot were the American farmers and the American consumers. The fact that this billion dollar grain robbery did not arouse vociferous and widespread indignation testifies to the relative eclipse of wheat as a critical element in our daily lives. (It may also bespeak our lack of moral and political vertebra as a nation.) See D. Morgan, *Merchants of Grain* (New York, 1979).

A recently-spotted American bumper sticker—our version of the wall poster—reads startlingly as an amalgamation of the old famine plot and the current oil plot themes: "Let Them Eat Oil." Reported by Paul Harvey, syndicated radio broadcast, 4 September 1979.

[63] Raunié, *Chansonnier historique*, 5: 272.

[64] Narbonne, *Journal*, p. 144. The rumor was perhaps unfounded, Narbonne remarked, but "it is still certain that ideas similar to it were in the air."

been part of the plot to poison the heirs of Louis XIV.[65] He was fiercely reviled as a "foutu malheureux," a "foutu bougre," and a "Jean Foutre" who shall be "punished by us, the people of France."[66] But in many ways the harshest and most telling epithet uttered against the prince-minister was that he was "a grain merchant."[67]

Bourbon's brusque dismissal in 1726 (along with the exile of his mistress, the Pâris brothers, and other members of their circle) was widely interpreted as confirmation of public suspicions of the famine plot.[68] Not even the duke's death mitigated the intensity of feeling about him. "The Prince will not be regretted by the public," Barbier observed, "he suffers a reproach that is not easily forgotten, that he made them eat exorbitantly-priced bread for a long time."[69] Bourbon had the misfortune to die in 1740 in the midst of another terrible scarcity, a coincidence that sharpened the collective memory of his atrocities. One of the most extensively circulated epitaphs read:

Cy-gist M. le duc de Bourbon
Prince d'assez mauvaise mine
Qui paie actuellement sur le charbon
Ce qu'il a pris sur la farine.[70]

This bit of highly charged verse remained alive till the end of the old regime, for it was cited as proof later in the century that the famine plot had long existed.[71] The idea that the dearth of 1725 had been an "artificial" one became entrenched in the minds of many Frenchmen.[72] Dubuisson, a Paris police commissaire around mid-century, recalled the scarcity as a needless and tragic one that had more to do with the "voracity" of Bourbon's entourage than with the inclemency of the weather.[73] Baron d'Holbach ascribed the dearth to a "monopoly" led by the chief minister and his mistress.[74] In 1770 Turgot denounced the "double monopoly" on the pur-

---

[65] Police report, ca. January 1726, MS. Bast. 10273.

[66] See Gazetins de police, ca. October 1726, MS. Bast. 10155 and police reports, ca. early 1726, MS. Bast. 10273.

[67] Gazetins de police, 2 June 1726, MS. Bast. 10156.

[68] See F. Funck-Brentano, ed., "Gazetins de police" (14–16 September 1740), in *Revue Rétrospective* (July–December 1887): 143.

[69] *Journal de Barbier* (ed. 1866), 3: 193 (January 1740).

[70] Gazetins de police, 13–15 February 1740, MS. Bast. 10167, fol. 30. For slight variations of the same verse, see Raunié, *Chansonnier historique*, 5: 272 and Schelle, ed., *Oeuvres de Turgot*, 2: 46–47.

[71] Leprévost de Beaumont, memorandum to king, 1777, in E. Le Mercier, *Le Prévot dit de Beaumont* (Bernay, 1883), pp. 303–304; Leprévost, *Dénonciation d'un pacte de famine générale au roi Louis XV* (Paris, n.d.), p. 22.

[72] See Saint-Simon, *Mémoires*, 17: 209–211 ("Ce manège des blés a paru une si bonne ressource, et si conforme à l'humanité et aux lumières de Mr le duc et des Pâris. . . ."); P.P.F.J.H. Lemercier de la Rivière, *L'Intérêt général de l'Etat* (Amsterdam, 1770), p. 269; P.J.A. Roubaud, *Représentations aux magistrats* (Paris, 1769), p. 412.

[73] Dubuisson to Caumont, 30 January 1740, in A. Rouxel, ed., *Lettres du commissaire Dubuisson au marquis de Caumont, 1735–1741* (Paris, 1882), p. 610.

[74] D'Holbach, *Système de la nature* (1780), 2: 289, cited by B. Willey, *The Eighteenth-Century Background* (Boston, 1961), p. 164.

chase (victimizing the *laboureurs*) and on the sale (victimizing the consumers) of grain exercised by Bourbon's provisioning company.[75] The secretary of one of the century's most durable ministers, Maurepas, blamed the duke and his financial advisers for having "established" the dearth of 1725 for their profit and that of the government.[76]

Well before the subsistence crisis of 1725, the duc de Bourbon's reputation had been seriously damaged by his liaison with Madame de Prie.[77] The mistresses of men in power in France have never won popularity contests, but it is hard to say precisely why this charming and intelligent woman was so ardently despised. She was denounced as an "adulteress," but this was not a title to which she had exclusive claim.[78] Perhaps it was resentment because she had all the qualities which the prince-minister lacked. Perhaps it was because she lacked the one quality he could boast: good birth. She came from a recently ennobled family of financiers. Her father, Berthelot de Pleneuf, one of the leading *intéressés* in Louis XIV's affairs and associate of the Pâris brothers, had been accused of perpetrating huge thefts as an army supplier: connections and suppositions that resurfaced in 1725.[79] She encouraged the duke to rely heavily on the Pâris brothers and she became known as their protector. Said to be driven by a boundless lust for power and wealth, Madame de Prie—she took the name from her husband, a titled ambassador who conveniently spent a great deal of time abroad—was frequently portrayed as the mastermind of the famine plot. According to one observer:

It's she who disposes of all the commissions [for the purchase and sale of grain] and who alone sustains those monsters [the Pâris brothers]. It is she who is most guilty of everything that afflicts the public, and everyone knows that she draws immense sums from everything, because of her pretty position as the whore of Monsieur le duc. A bitch like this one ought to have her womb slit open from top to bottom.[80]

The dearth of 1725 featured another leading lady whose virtues, contrasted with the vices of Madame de Prie, thrust the latter's infamy into stark relief. She was St. Genevieve, patroness of the capital even as Madame de Prie was its nemesis. Ever since she saved Paris from famine centuries before she had been the object of a popular cult. In times of distress, especially subsistence-related difficulties, Parisians appealed for her intercession.[81] In 1725 her *châsse*, or reliquary, was "descended", or taken down, from its niche in the church that bore her name and paraded through the

---

[75] Turgot, "Septième lettre sur le commerce des grains," 2 December 1770, in *Oeuvres de Turgot*, 3: 324.

[76] Sale, ed., *Mémoires du comte de Maurepas* (Paris, 1792), 2: 171n.

[77] L.E.A. Jobez, *La France sous Louis XV, 1715–74* (Paris 1864–1873), 2: 348–349.

[78] Duclos, *Mémoires secrets*, 77: 31.

[79] Thirion, *Prie*, pp. xx, 1–3, 55.

[80] Gazetins de police, 24 August 1725, MS. Bast. 10155, fols. 52–53. For a defense of Mme. de Prie against charges of avarice and prodigality, see Thirion, *Prie*, pp. 325ff.

[81] See my "Religion, Subsistence and Social Control: the Uses of Saint Genevieve," *Eighteenth-Century Studies*, 13 (1979/80): 142–168.

city in a propitiatory rite that commanded massive popular participation. The sacred and the profane alternatives were commingled in a riddle that circulated at the time:

> On demande quelle différence il y a entre Mme de Prie
> et la châsse de Ste Geneviève . . .
> C'est que pour obtenir des grâces de Ste Geneviève
> il faut la descendre et pour en obtenir de Mme de Prie
> il faut la monter.[82]

In a piece of verse that also gained currency at this time, Madame de Prie is made to rebuke St. Genevieve for infringing upon what the duke's mistress now claims as her bailiwick:

> A la patronne de Paris
> la de Prie a dit en colère:
> Demeurez dans votre taudis,
> Sans vous mêler de mes affaires;
> Sachez que c'est moi à présent
> Qui fait la pluie et le beau temps.[83]

Madame de Prie's orders were carried out by the lieutenant general of police, Ravot d'Ombreval, who, it was said, "belonged" to her.[84] In fact they were relatives and it is quite likely that he received his appointment because the duke and de Prie wanted someone upon whom they could count absolutely in that highly sensitive post.[85] D'Ombreval had been a magistrate in the cour des aides where he came to know the financial milieu and allegedly developed mutually profitable bonds with certain farmers-general.[86] No high official was more closely concerned with day-to-day provisioning affairs than the lieutenant general. During the subsistence crises of 1693, 1699, and 1709, the first two lieutenants of police, La Reynie and d'Argenson, had earned reputations for genuine devotion to the consumer interest. In the eyes of many Parisians, d'Ombreval betrayed his office by using his position as a cover for the grain "manège" whose field operations he personally directed.[87]

D'Ombreval's ineptitude in dealing with public opinion heightened popular suspicion and alienation. Confronted at the Halle by a mother who

---

[82] Raunié, *Chansonnier historique*, 5: 59.

[83] Ibid, 5: 58. Cf. Duclos, *Mémoires secrets*, 77: 31.

[84] Thirion, *Prie*, pp. 61, 103.

[85] Narbonne wrote that Prie was d'Ombreval's brother, but that is surely incorrect. *Journal*, p. 143. M. Chassaigne had them as cousins. *La Lieutenance générale de police de Paris* (Paris, 1906), p. 60. But if Thirion's family tree is right, then d'Ombreval was the husband of the sister of Prie's father and thus her uncle by marriage. Thirion, *Prie*, p. 4.

[86] 28 August 1725, MS. Bast. 10270.

[87] Anon., "Histoire de ce qui s'est passé au sujet des bleds en 1725," MS. 3308, Arsenal; Gazetins de police, 28 September 1725, MS. Bast. 10155, fols. 78–79; *Journal de Barbier* (ed. 1858), 1: 402–404 (August 1725). "Tu nous empoissonnes le pain, tu nous attaques par la faim" went a contemporary verse. Raunié, *Chansonnier historique*, 5: 79. Another line described him as "ce vil proconsul, cet oppresseur de l'innocence." Ibid., p. 84.

complained that she could not feed her children "since the price of bread is out of reach," he advised: "Let them eat cabbage runts," a remark less poetic than the one attributed years later to Marie-Antoinette but no less callous and provocative.[88] The lieutenant general presided over the public executions of the instigators of the Faubourg St.-Antoine bread riot.[89] Furiously assailed in the marketplaces and taverns, he was physically threatened with mob violence when he showed himself in the streets.[90] In late August the duke dismissed him, offering him up as a sacrifice to public opinion in the hope that Paris would be appeased by this gesture. His departure was applauded, but it was not very reassuring because no one doubted that the source of the evil was to be found above his head.[91] The news that d'Ombreval had in fact not been disgraced but merely transferred to the intendancy of Tours made Parisians even more cynical. They did not feel fully avenged until the ex-lieutenant of police was recalled and exiled with the others in the duke's entourage the following year by Louis XV and Fleury.[92]

One of the scurrilous verses abroad in 1725 went:

Nous voyons le duc de Bourbon
Monté dessus son char de prix [Prie]
Trainé par les 4 paris.[93]

The four Pâris who pulled the duke's chariot were brothers, members of a humble provincial family who enjoyed a startling rise to wealth and power.[94] Unlike many of the great financial families, which began in banking and turned to provisioning affairs only rarely, in response to urgent ministerial pleas, the Pâris started out in grain and other basic supplies and then gravitated imperceptibly to money and credit management. Contracts for army provisioning launched their public career and they remained

---

[88] Anon., "Histoire de ce qui s'est passé," MS. 3308, Arsenal.

[89] July 1725, MS. Bast. 10270.

[90] Gazetins de police, 23, 25 August 1725, MS. Bast. 10155, fols. 51–52, 55.

[91] Archives de la Préfecture de Police, AB/96, fol. 173; Gazetins de police, 25 August 1725, MS. Bast. 10155, fols. 53–54. Wrote Barbier: "Un lieutenant de police ne pourroit pas faire ce manège-là huit jours s'il n'étoit soutenu du ministère. Ils ont voulu tirer de l'argent; et après l'avoir fait, on sacrifie politiquement le lieutenant général de police, pour faire tomber sur lui l'iniquité." Journal de Barbier (ed. 1858), 1: 405.

[92] CG to d'Ombreval, 11 August 1726, G⁷ 37; Journal de Barbier (ed. 1866), 1: 429 (June 1726). Narbonne heard a rumor that d'Ombreval had fled to England "with considerable sums" from his grain "maneuvers." Journal, p. 138. As late as 1738 there were still reports that the parlement was going to investigate his role in the subsistence crisis of 1725 and that he would be forced to abandon his mastership of requests. Gazetins de police, 7 January 1728, MS. Bast. 10158, fols. 8–9. J. Peuchet claimed that d'Ombreval had kept "his dignity and integrity" during his brief tenure as police chief. Mémoires tirés de la police de Paris (Paris, 1838), pp. 274–279.

[93] Raunié, Chansonnier historique, 5: 54.

[94] On their origins, see Saint-Simon, Mémoires, 37: 183–86 and R. Dubois-Corneau, Pâris de Montmartel (Paris, 1917). A modern biographical study of the brothers is desperately needed. There is a useful but rapid sketch in G. Chaussinand-Nogaret, Gens de finance au 18e siècle (Paris, 1972), chaps. 1 and 2.

deeply involved in *vivres* for more than a half century.[95] It is likely that they participated in the massive civil provisioning operations undertaken to meet near-famine conditions in 1709.[96] The brothers served as advisers to Louis XIV's last controller-general and to the Regency's council on finances. Displaced by John Law, they worked discreetly to undermine the "System" and returned to power in the wake of its collapse as the kitchen cabinet of Controller-General Dodun.[97]

The Pâris brothers were perceived as playing a no less important role in the famine plot than Samuel Bernard. "It is said aloud," Barbier related, "that M. le duc has made a contract with the Pâris to buy all the grain in the kingdom while it is still in the ground."[98] They were alleged to have made, along with Bernard, over 25,000,000 livres in speculative profits by mid-August.[99] While it is clear that the brothers neither monopolized futures nor reaped such outlandish profits, it is true that they made purchases directly in behalf of the government in addition to helping Dodun shape the global subsistence strategy in collaboration with Bernard. While Bernard specialized in importing foreign grain, the Pâris appear to have focused on marshaling domestic surpluses.[100]

The fact that their chief buying agent was François Poisson enabled or invited certain contemporaries later in the century to widen the burgeoning conspiratorial web. For Poisson was the father of the future royal mistress-counselor Pompadour. Like Madame de Prie, she grew up in the financial-

---

[95] Duclos, *Mémoires secrets sur le règne de Louis XIV, la régence, et le règne de Louis XV* (Paris, 1864), 2: 282; Pâris Duverney to Orry, 28 November 1744, G⁷ 61, ÁN; F¹² 647, AN; L. Dussieux and E. Soulié, *Mémoires du duc de Luynes sur la cour de Louis XV (1735-1758)* (Paris, 1860), 4: 195 (July 1742); F. M. Grimm, *Correspondence littéraire, philosophique, et critique par Grimm, Diderot, Raynal, Meister, etc.*, ed. by M. Tourneux (Paris, 1877-1882), 9: 105-106 (August 1770); *Encyclopédie Méthodique*, "art militaire" (Paris, 1787), 3: 285-286. Duverney sported the sobriquet "flour general." F. Barrière, ed., *Mémoires de Madame du Hausset* (Paris, 1846), p. 126. Duverney helped Voltaire to make his fortune through the *vivres*. See, for example, Voltaire to Duverney, 15 October 1750, in T. Besterman, ed., *Voltaire's Correspondence* (Geneva, 1953-61), 18: 183-184 (#3670).

[96] A. M. de Boislisle, "Le Grand hiver et la disette de 1709," *Revue des questions historiques*, 73 (1903): 472.

[97] *Mémoires de Maurepas*, 2: 49-52. See also M. Marion, "Un essai de politique sociale en 1724," *Revue du dix-huitième siècle*, 1 (1913): 33.

[98] *Journal de Barbier* (ed. 1866), 1: 430 (June 1726); Thirion, *Prie*, p. 236. See also 27 August 1725, MS. Bast. 10270.

[99] Gazetins de police, 23 August 1725, MS. Bast. 10155. Others reported that the Pâris brothers made as much as 500,000 livres in a single day. Narbonne, *Journal*, p. 143.

[100] Pâris La Montagne to CG, 25 February 1726, and memorandums of 5, 13 February 1726, G⁷ 1660-1665, AN. In September Poisson was prepared to procure up to 10,000 muids, probably from Auvergne and Dauphiné—a staggering quantity representing between one-eighth and one-ninth of total annual Parisian consumption. CG to PG, 25 September 1725, Coll. JF 1117, fol. 217. See also Coll. JF 1116, fol. 31. It is interesting to note that the alleged profiteer, Pâris La Montagne, made a strong case for using a *régie* rather than a contractual entrepreneur on the grounds that it was cheaper for the king and more likely to result in high quality merchandise. Memorandum, 13 February 1726, G⁷ 1660-1665, AN. Samuel Bernard was not the "father and creator" of the Pâris brothers, as Michelet contended, but he did have close political and business relations with them. J. Michelet, *Histoire de France*, in *Oeuvres complètes* (Paris, 1897), 15: 23n, 26; Dubois Corneau, *Pâris*, p. 117; Narbonne, *Journal*, p. 296.

provisioning milieu. Pâris-Monmartel was her godfather, as well as one of her mother's most persistent lovers. She married the nephew of another of her mother's suitors, the farmer-general Le Normant de Tournehem, who also appears to have supplied the capital with emergency grain in 1725. Upon the fall of the Pâris brothers with the duke's entourage in 1726, Poisson was condemned—to be hanged, according to contemporaries—for having embezzled some 230,000 livres from the grain contracts: another striking vindication of those who believed in the famine plot. Poisson fled the country and later was fully rehabilitated and even rewarded for service to the nation, once his daughter achieved power.[101]

The most remarkable thing about the Pâris brothers was their capacity to recover. Exiled with the others in June 1726 (DuVerney even spent some time in the Bastille for a case of malversation that was ostensibly not grain-related), the brothers suffered eclipse for only a few years.[102] The famine plot stigma obliged them to behave more discreetly when they returned to influence. But they came to be regarded by the elite as "the most esteemed persons in the realm, the eldest [Monmartel] for finances, DuVerney for war."[103] One observer characterized the brothers as constituting "the soul" of the contrôle-général from 1730 to 1760 and the chief reason that Monmartel did not assume the post himself may have been the sinister memories of 1725.[104]

If Controller-General Dodun did not attain the unpopularity of the Pâris, it was because he was viewed as nothing more than their "tool."[105] He was the "deceiver" and the "veritable Turk" whose mission it was to mislead

---

[101] Dubois-Corneau, *Pâris*, pp. 125–126; P. de Nolhac, *Louis XV et Madame de Pompadour* (Paris, 1904), pp. 22–25; *Mémoires de Luynes*, 7: 67–69 (September 1745); Marville to Maurepas, 6 May 1745, in A. de Boislisle, ed., *Lettres de M. de Marville, lieutenant général de police, au ministre Maurepas (1742–1747)* (Paris, 1895–1905), 2: 71. Upon his rehabilitation, Poisson again undertook victualing tasks for the government. Nolhac, *Pompadour*, pp. 25–31 and *Mémoires de Luynes*, 11: 86 (19 March 1751). On Lenormant's provisioning role, see (?) to Hérault, 8 January 1726, MS. Bast. 10272.

[102] For the exile orders, see 6, 12, 24 June 1726, O¹ 373, AN. Narbonne claimed that Bourbon alerted the brothers in time to allow them to burn all compromising papers. *Journal*, 147–148. On Duverney's incarceration, see 13 September 1726, MS. Bast. 10949 and *Journal de Barbier* (ed. 1858), 1: 429, 441. Even in prison or exile, Duverney was kept informed on grain shipments and prices in the capital. PG to Duverney, 15 February, 22 March 1726, Coll. JF 1118, fols. 72, 102.

[103] Duc de Croy, *Journal inédit du duc de Croy, 1718–1784*, ed. by de Grouchy and P. Cottin (Paris, 1906–1907), 1: 69 (January 1747). In Turgot's imaginary bookshelf there was a book ascribed to the Pâris brothers entitled "Véritable utilité de la guerre." *Oeuvres de Turgot*, 3: 686.

[104] To the Earl of B . . . , letter VI, R. Talbot, *Letters on the French Nation Considered in the Different Departments* (London, 1771), 1: 59–60; Marville to Maurepas, 9 September 1745 and 12 November 1746, *Lettres de Marville*, 2: 153 and 3: 62–63; Voltaire to Louis Gaspard Fabry, 30 November 1759 and to J. R. Tronchin, 30 November 1759, in *Voltaire's Correspondence*, 37: 245–246 (nos. 7893 and 7894); René-Louis de Voyer, Marquis d'Argenson, *Journal et mémoires*, ed. by E. J. B. Rathery (Paris, 1859–1867), 3: 179–180 (29 September, 12 October 1747), 229 (19 December 1748), 245 (20 February 1749). See also the laudatory evaluations of the Pâris as statesmen by Voltaire and Forbonnais. Voltaire, *Observations sur MM. Jean Lass, Melon et Dutot sur le commerce, le luxe, les monnaies et les impôts* (1738), in *Oeuvres complètes* (Paris, 1879), 22: 365 and F. Veron de Forbonnais, *Recherches et considérations sur les finances de France depuis 1595 jusqu'en 1721* (Liège, 1758), 5: 295.

[105] July 1725, MS. Bast. 10270. See also Marquis d'Argenson, ed., *Mémoires et journal inédit du marquis d'Argenson* (Paris, 1857–1858), 1: 24 and H. Martin, *Histoire de France* (Paris, 1859), 15: 126.

the public and to provide a cover for the machinations of the grain cabal. He provided the passports for grain removals, arranged transportation and storage, and, it was charged, kept local officials quiet through a blend of bribery and intimidation.[106] For a number of reasons public opinion was hostile to him even before the crystallization of the famine plot persuasion. He inaugurated a brutal deflationary policy in 1724 meant to reduce both prices and wages. Workers heatedly resisted the mandated cutbacks and there was considerable labor unrest in the capital in 1724 and 1725.[107] Just about the time that the dearth began to be felt, Dodun announced the levying of a new 2 percent tax in kind called the *cinquantième* as well as the traditional confirmation-of-privileges tax marking the ascension of a new monarch. Though these imposts did not directly touch the majority of Parisians, they aroused far-reaching opposition as reminders of government mismanagement, avidity, and despotism. Member of a relatively new "robe" noble family enriched *dans les finances*, Dodun was scorned for his vanity and parvenu manner.[108] "It is said," wrote Barbier at the moment of Dodun's fall, "that no minister has ever pillaged as much as this one."[109] His dismissal, too, was viewed as tacit admission by the young king of the existence of a plot.

We have already had a glimpse of the preeminent part played by Samuel Bernard in the famine plot persuasion. He earned his millions, Narbonne affirmed, "from the Jew trade."[110] In fact, though it is true he was a money-lender, he owed his success originally to the Protestant diaspora in the years after the revocation of the Edict of Nantes and he constituted an international network of associates, many of whom were his own relatives.[111] The government called upon him in the 1690s for myriad financial, commercial, and victualing operations and by the time of the War of Spanish Succession, Bernard had assumed almost exclusive control of French foreign exchange. He had become indispensable to the government and he knew it. Once humble and even obsequious in his relations with ministers, his manner turned to swagger and insolence. His power—fruit of the first triumph of new-style banking over the old-fashioned finance—troubled contemporaries precisely because it was not based on the familiar model of the opulent tax farmer or *traitant*.[112]

---

[106] Gazetins de police, 23 August 1725, MS. Bast. 10155, fol. 51 and police report, 5 September 1725, MS. Bast. 10270.

[107] A. Babeau, *La Lutte de l'Etat contre la cherté en 1724* (Paris, 1892); M. Marion, "Un Essai de politique sociale," 28–42; S. L. Kaplan, "Réflexions sur la police du monde du travail, 1700–1815," *Revue historique*, 261 (1979): 17–77.

[108] F. Bluche, *L'Origine des magistrats du Parlement de Paris au 18e siècle*, in *Mémoires de la Fédération des sociétés historiques et archéologiques de Paris et de l'Ile-de-France*, 5–6 (1956 for 1953–1954): 150–51; Marais, *Journal*, 3: 154 (February 1725); *Mémoires de Maurepas*, 2: 53–56. "Galonnez, galonnez, galonnez-moi car je suis bon gentilhomme," Dodun exhorted his tailor in a burlesque reported by Marais, *Journal*, 3: 154.

[109] *Journal de Barbier* (ed. 1858), 1: 429 (June 1726).

[110] Narbonne, *Journal*, pp. 412–413.

[111] L. Rothkrug, *Opposition to Louis XIV: The Political and Social Origins of the French Enlightenment* (Princeton, 1965), pp. 400–403.

[112] Lüthy, *Banque*, 1: 121–125 and *passim*; J. Saint-Germain, *Samuel Bernard. Le Banquier des rois* (Paris, 1960).

Given Bernard's enormous wealth and influence, his close relationship with previous controllers-general, and the experience in provisioning the capital that he had acquired during the dearths of the 1690s, it was natural for Dodun to turn to him on the eve of difficulties in 1724.[113] Though Bernard was not the government's sole supplier, there is no doubt that he was the preeminent one in 1725–1726. It is likely that he imported over 40,000 muids of grain, representing colossal advances of at least ten to fifteen million livres.[114] Faced with other pressing obligations, Dodun was slow in making payments to Bernard; indeed, as rumor had it, the government may already have been in debt to Bernard for services rendered prior to the dearth (thus explaining, in the minds of certain contemporaries, why the banker was "rewarded" with the "grain monopoly").[115] But the beauty of dealing with Bernard was that he was a very patient man: every delay in reimbursement merely compounded the interest charges. Yet he knew how to mix charity with business. In September 1725 he granted the Parisian municipality an interest-free million-livre loan for the purchase of grain.[116] What would believers in the famine plot have thought had they known that it was also Bernard who lent Hérault enough money to purchase the post of lieutenant of police and replace d'Ombreval.[117]

Whereas the Pâris brothers were merely resilient, Bernard proved to be indestructible. Though he was as deeply implicated as the others in the alleged conspiracy, he was the only one not to suffer even momentary disgrace.[118] Apparently it was thought that the fall of the others would mollify opinion. While the Pâris, Dodun, the duc de Bourbon, and Madame de Prie received *lettres de cachet*, Bernard received "a very gracious letter" from Cardinal Fleury, the new leading minister, celebrating Bernard's attachment to the king and his devotion to the state.[119] Bernard was retained because he was needed, and the government continued to use him not merely in financial affairs but in provisioning, despite the stigma of the famine plot. In 1731–1732, Bernard imported at least 5,000 muids and per-

---

[113] On his early provisioning experience, see Saint-Germain, *Bernard*, pp. 39–51, 282 and G⁷ 1637, AN.

[114] One report indicated that Bernard had 40,000 muids on the way as of January 1726. But he had imported *at least* 10,000 muids in 1725. Coll. JF 1117, fol. 25. He also supplied over a half million livres' worth to the Hôpital Général. PG to CG, 20 December 1732, Coll. JF 121, fols. 25–26. In addition, Bernard imported rice and furnished beef. Assemblée de police, 27 December 1725, Coll. JF 1117, fol. 64 and CG to LG, 25 March 1725, G⁷ 34, AN.

[115] CG to Bernard, 24 September, 29 October 1725, G⁷ 34, AN.

[116] Marais to Bouhier, 20 September 1725 in Marais *Journal*, 3: 363; Maurepas to PG, 14 September 1725, Coll. JF 1116, fol. 285. The municipality arranged many relatively modest grain deals, including the importation of American wheat. 10 March 1726, MS. Bast. 10156, fol. 103.

[117] Fonds Feydeau de Brou, DE¹ article 4, Archives Seine-Paris.

[118] On the suspicions and denunciation of Bernard, see above pp. 9–13 and Gazetins de police, MS. Bast. 10156, fols. 54–55; Anon., "Histoire de ce qui s'est passé au sujet des bleds," MS. 3308, Arsenal; Anon., "Histoire de ce qui s'est passé," 9 October 1725, MS. Bast. 10033.

[119] Marais to Bouhier, 18 June 1726 in Marais, *Journal*, 3: 429. Cardinal Fleury also honored him upon his death. *Mercure suisse* (January 1739), 21–22.

haps as much as 10,000 muids.[120] He remained his haughty self, but this
time he had to deal with a much more exigent controller-general, Orry.[121]
Bernard demanded indemnities for losses that Orry esteemed "excessive"
and, in addition, failed to provide all the records demanded by the controller-general. Orry warned that he would not reimburse him until he had
investigated the enterprise meticulously: "I do not say that we lay the blame
on you for these losses, but we must look into things and understand them,
for that is my way of doing things and I will not change."[122] Had Bernard
not died in 1739, on the eve of the next great dearth, perhaps he would
have vented his bile by refusing to assist the controller-general in mobilizing emergency supplies. In any event, his erstwhile collaborators, the
Pâris brothers, later avenged him by forcing Orry's dismissal in the mid-
forties.

In referring to Bernard or the Pâris, contemporaries often spoke of
"Messrs. des Finances" or "the Bank."[123] The assumption was of a tentacular
yet monolithic creature, and it provoked something like the hysteria
aroused by the "monster" bank of the Jacksonian period in America. We
know of course that there was no *union des classes* in the financial milieu,
but it is worth pointing out that, in addition to Bernard and the Pâris
brothers, there were other bankers and/or financiers involved in supply
operations in 1725-1726. We have already come upon the farmer-general
Le Normant de Tournehem. One of his relatives and correspondents, a
receiver of the *taille* in Auvergne, was also engaged in finding grain for
the capital.[124] The Paris banker Delarue purchased flour at the king's
request.[125] Robert Arbuthnot, a "Mississippien," a commercial agent at
Rouen for many English houses, and later a Paris banker, imported Baltic
wheat.[126] "I would like to be able to contribute in some way to procuring
grain abundance in this city [Paris] wrote the banker Pierre Nolasque
Couvay to Hérault in 1725, and in the course of the year he arranged
imports from Holland and England.[127] The "bank" continued to play an

---

[120] CG to de Gasville, 19 May 1731, G⁷ 46, AN; CG to Bernard, 24 May 1732, G⁷ 47, AN;
Assemblée de Police, 21, 26 June 1731, MS. fr. 11356, fols. 166–169, BN.

[121] See Bernard's tirade against certain local officials who got in his way: "Je serois bien
malheureux de me donner tant de peine pour servir mon Prince et ma Patrie et estre barré
par ces sortes de gens." To Hérault, 6 July 1731, MS. Bast. 10275.

[122] CG to Bernard, 24 May 1732, G⁷ 47, AN. This despite the Polish schnaps Bernard gave
to Orry. 19 May 1731, G⁷ 46, AN.

[123] Saint-Simon, cited by Chassin, *Les Elections et les Cahiers*, 4: 105; d'Argenson, *Journal*, ed.
by Rathery, 7: 286 (27 August 1752); Gazetins de police, 25 August 1725, MS. Bast. 10155, fols.
53–54. Most contemporaries were much less aware of the discontinuity between "les financiers"
and "la banque" than is Lüthy. *Banque*, 1.

[124] De la Grandville to Hérault, 14 December 1725, MS. Bast. 10271.

[125] CG to LG, 3 December 1725, ibid.

[126] CG to PG, 8 September 1725, Coll. JF 1117, fol. 195; Arbuthnot to PG, 23 September 1725,
ibid., fols 227–228. See also Lüthy, *Banque* 1: 348, 426 and 2: 316.

[127] CG to LG, 20 November 1725, G⁷ 34, AN; Couvay to LG, 17 October 1725, MS. Bast. 10274.
See also Lüthy, *Banque*, 2: 788 and P. Harsin, "La Création de la Compagnie d'occident," *Revue
d'histoire économique et sociale*, 34 (1956): 7–42.

important role in emergency provisioning until the end of the century. One encounters, among others, Thellusson, Pictet, Van Robais, Babaud, Goosens, Bouret, Grand.[128]

Another party commonly associated with the famine plot was the Company of the Indies, an international trading corporation with whose reorganization Bernard had been deeply involved in the 1690s.[129] Like the "bank," it loomed as a sort of ubiquitous monster, a semi-private, semi-public cover for illicit operations in both the public and private sectors whose frontier was radically blurred. "As long as the Company of the Indies exists," consumers in the marketplaces were "murmuring" in November 1725, "bread will be expensive."[130] It was charged that the agents of the Company, operating on the orders of Bourbon and the Pâris, scoured the countryside for new grain to prevent it from reaching the market, attempted to pass off old domestic grain as foreign merchandise, and tried to force rotten grain on the bakers.[131]

In fact the Company of the Indies did engage in grain importation for the government—probably many thousands of muids.[132] Laurent, named by d'Ombreval to serve as the Company's Parisian correspondent, was a grain merchant who served as a supplier to the Hôtel-Dieu and was probably a member of the family that did that hospital's milling and that furnished the Invalides with bread.[133] Theoretically, Laurent was supposed to do nothing more than sell the grain delivered by the Company, but it is clear that he engaged in widespread domestic buying operations on his own and in association with several other merchants.[134] He may very well have done his buying under the banner of the Company, in the hope that he could gain certain competitive advantages by brandishing the Company's colors in the eyes of local officials and dealers. Such indiscretion might very well have led to panicky reports that the Company was hoarding grain everywhere.

Laurent soon found himself in trouble, though not for his depredations in the realm of public opinion. He quarreled with one of his associates,

[128] MS. Bast. 10274–10277; Thellusson to PG, 29 October 1740, Coll. JF 1109, fol. 53; Lüthy, *Banque*, 2: 149, 195–201, 321–324, 354–355, 452; P. Dardel, *Navires et marchandises dans les ports de Rouen et du Havre au XVIIIe siècle* (Paris, 1963), p. 406; M. Marion, "Une famine en Guyenne (1747–1748)," *Revue historique*, 66 (May–August 1891): 241–287; Marion, *Histoire financière de la France depuis 1715* (Paris, 1914–1927), 1: 276; *Recueil des principales lois relatives au commerce des grains* (Paris, 1769), p. 98; J. B. L. Coquereau, *Mémoires concernant l'administration des finances sous le ministère de M. l'abbé Terrai* (London, 1776), p. 199.

[129] Saint-Germain, *Bernard*, p. 26–30. The duc de Bourbon was also known to be a protector of the Indies Company. Lüthy, *Banque*, 1: 416.

[130] 24 November 1725, MS. Bast. 10271.

[131] Gazetins de police, 26 September, 15 November 1725, MS. Bast. 10155, fols. 70, 136, and 10 March 1726, MS. Bast. 10136, fol. 103. "Putrid flour" was allegedly given to priests to distribute to the indigent or used for soldiers' bread. 23 March 1726, MS. Bast. 10156, fol. 121.

[132] Coll. JF 1116, fols. 67–68; LG to prévôt des marchands, 9 January 1725, F[11] 264.

[133] Deliberations of bureau of Hôtel-Dieu, 5 October 1725, AAP, no. 94 and D5B⁶ 1814, Arch. Seine-Paris.

[134] De Gasville to PG, 3 September, August 1725, Coll. JF 1117, fols. 82–83, 85; Lambert to PG, 1 September 1725, ibid., fol. 84 bis.

against whom he sought a *lettre de cachet*.[135] The Company complained that Laurent refused to present his books for scrutiny.[136] And he suffered the fate of many eighteenth-century victualers: after the ministry that had hired him fell, the new government arbitrarily reduced his promised commission by one-third.[137] These mini-*visas* were viewed as proof that some sort of plot had indeed existed. The events of 1725–1726 barely affected the Company of the Indies. It continued to import grain when the government requested its "extraordinary" aid and the collective memory of its alleged perfidies remained alive throughout the century.[138]

Kept abreast by daily intelligence reports, the authorities were keenly aware of the proliferation of suspicions and rumors implicating the highest officials in antisocial conspiracies. Dodun himself worried about how to respond to the gossip "that we used our authority to prevent grain owners from marketing grain in Paris in order to be in a position to sell the king's grain at the price that suited us."[139] In fact the government neither addressed the issues raised by these rumors nor developed a policy for dealing with public opinion. The presumption seemed to have been that open discussion of the accusations, so long as prices were high and consumers uneasy, would only serve to give them a certain credence.

A local official like Narbonne understood that to demand explanations was a vain and dangerous business: "It is a mystery that is difficult to penetrate and that it is prudent not to examine more closely."[140] In late September the future Cardinal Fleury wrote Hérault:

A man of the first consideration at Court told me yesterday that a person named Bonnet shipped in wheat from Rouen that had cost him 22 livres the septier and on which he was willing to earn only 8 livres [!]. The police commissaires made him sell it at 42 livres. I don't believe any of it. But it is grievous that rumors against the government are increasing instead of decreasing and that this diminishes confidence and circulation more and more.[141]

Not long after this letter Fleury was apparently placed under a kind of house arrest ("for having told the king about the misery of the people," according to the very rumors about which he was alarmed), even as the young duc de Gesvres was exiled to the country for having protested the continuing dearth to Bourbon.[142] An individual who sent the ministry sensitive information that he had uncovered concerning the location of two large grain hoards was given forty-eight hours to leave the kingdom, ac-

---

[135] MS. Bast. 10271.

[136] Memorandum to Hérault, 25 October 1725, ibid.

[137] Memorandum, 4 September 1727, ibid.

[138] For examples of the Company's purchases, see C. 2677, AD Calvados and J. Letacannoux, *Les Subsistances et le commerce des grains en Bretagne au XVIIIe siècle* (Rennes, 1909), p. 167.

[139] CG to Bernard, early 1726, cited by Saint-Germain, *Bernard*, 51. Cf. CG to Bernard, 18 October 1725, G⁷ 35, AN for a similar expression of anxiety about public opinion.

[140] Narbonne, *Journal*, p. 138.

[141] Fréjus to Hérault, 26 September 1725, MS. Bast. 10270.

[142] Gazetins de police, 24 December 1725, MS. Bast. 10155, fols. 181–182. Cf. Thirion, *Prie*, pp. 263–264.

cording to another source.[143] The government's refusal to investigate the plot, even after the cascade of dismissals, merely reinforced the conviction that there was something to hide.[144] Continued imports and a harvest that was reasonably good helped to dissipate, not the preoccupation with subsistence, but the obsession with plots and maneuvers—for the moment.

Though the next decade was marked by relative tranquillity over subsistence, there were moments of malaise, both for the authorities and the consumers. Bad auguries for the harvest caused prices to rise in May and June 1729. Even as Parisians shuddered at the prospect of another "test of hunger" and conjectured that there must be "some evil maneuver behind it from the court," so the Assembly of Police took pains to make sure that emergency provisioning operations "did not give the people cause to say that suppliers are hoarding grain in the king's name."[145] Fear of triggering another outbreak of rumors seemed to make the authorities reluctant to act decisively, reinforcing what I have elsewhere called the paralysis of discretion.[146] Nevertheless, the fresh scars of 1725–1726 did not keep the Assembly from commissioning at least a million livres' worth of wheat imports from Samuel Bernard when a spring drought menaced the 1731 harvest.[147] There appears to have been no public outcry because the harvest turned out to be excellent and the government did not have to flood the markets with foreign grain.[148]

---

[143] Anon., "Histoire de ce qui s'est passé au sujet des bleds en 1725," MS. 3308, Arsenal.

[144] Narbonne wondered whether Fleury, the new prime minister in fact if not in name, "feared to find proof of a too devastating nature of the bad administration" of Bourbon and the Pâris brothers. Journal, p. 147–148. See also Barbier who demanded "vengeance" for Parisians. Journal (ed. 1866), 1: 441–442 (August 1726). Parisians lit feux de joie to celebrate the downfall of the plotters. Dubois-Corneau, Pâris, 100. An "allegory" circulated in honor of the new ministry: "Le 11 juin 1726 mardi de la Pentecôte il est arrivé un terrible orage en France, qui est tombé sur le Dos d'un [Dodun] B[ourbon]. Pour éviter un pareil accident, on a établi Des Forts [name of new controller-general] dans le royaume; maintenant le royaume est si Fleury qu'il n'a plus de Prie." Mémoires de Maurepas, 2: 76.

[145] Gazetins de police, 5 May, 20 June 1729, MS. Bast. 10159, fols. 200, 228; Assemblée de Police, 26 May 1729, MS. fr. 11356, fol. 101, BN. See also the Assembly's sensitivity to the famine plot persuasion in 2 December 1728, ibid., fol. 62 and the sarcastic appreciation of a celebration in the king's honor in Gazetins, 28 November 1729, MS. Bast. 10160, fol. 140.

[146] See Kaplan, Bread, Politics and Political Economy, 1: 78 and 2: 546, 693.

[147] CG to de Gasville, 19 May 1731, G⁷ 46, AN; CG to Bernard, 24 May 1731, G⁷ 47, AN; Bernard to LG, 6 July 1731, MS. Bast. 10275; Assemblée de Police, 21 June 1731, MS. fr. 11356, fols. 166–167, BN.

[148] Assemblée de Police, 7 June, 19 July 1731, MS. fr. 11356, fols. 163, 170, BN; CG to Bernard, 14 May 1732, G⁷ 47, AN.

II. The Dearths of 1738-1741

Beginning in 1738, however, France suffered a series of grave subsistence crises that engulfed close to half the kingdom during the next four years and that recalled the desolation of 1709.[149] The harvest of 1738 was a catastrophe in the west; in the Paris region it was mediocre at best.[150] The following year's crop was highly uneven, yielding far too little to make up the deficits or to break the dearth momentum.[151] The 1740 harvest was a widespread disaster, producing in many places between a third and a half of "an ordinary year."[152] Speculative pressures and harassment by local police and consumer vigilantes disorganized the grain trade. Grain and flour prices in the capital and the Paris region more than doubled between December 1737 and the same month in 1740.[153] On several occasions the loaf of common bread in Paris climbed to 5 sous a pound, more than twice its "normal" price.[154] Acute subsistence crisis led inexorably

---

[149] Many contemporaries characterized the crises of 1738-1741 as worse than that of 1709. See subdelegates at Saumur and Tours to PG, 23 and 31 May 1739, Coll. JF 1120, fols. 188-189, 201-203. The authorities studied the measures taken in 1709 as potential models for 1740. See 27 October 1740, Conseil Secret, X¹ᵃ 8468, fol. 161, AN; CG to PG, 19 July 1740, Coll. JF 1121, fols. 83-84; Coll. JF 1111, fol. 73, and 1123, fol. 63. Saint-Simon drafted his memoirs for 1709 in 1740 and his description of it may very well have been colored by his more recent crisis experience. See Boislisle, "Le Grand hiver," pp. 447-448.

[150] Assemblées de Police, 26 June, 31 July, 28 August, 4 December 1738, MS. fr. 11356, fols. 351, 360, 365, 371, BN; M. Bricourt, M. Lachiver, and J. Queruel, "La Crise de subsistance des années 1740 dans le ressort du Parlement de Paris," Annales de Démographie historique (1974): 284-287.

[151] D'Argenson, Journal, ed. by Rathery, 2: 194 (July 1739); subdelegate of Dreux to PG, 27 June 1739, Coll. JF 1120, fols. 138-139; subdelegate of Meaux to PG, 8 July 1739, Coll. JF 1120, fols. 162-163; Assemblée de Police, 10 December 1739, MS. fr. 11356, fols. 406-407, BN; Foucaud to PG, 21 August 1739, Coll. JF 1119, fols. 32-33; Foucaud to LG, 30 September 1739, MS. Bast. 10277. I believe that Bricourt et al. are excessively sanguine about the 1739 harvest. "La Crise de subsistance des années 1740," p. 304.

[152] Lorcheres to CG, 1 July 1740, MS. Bast. 10006, fol. 288; Maurepas to Marville, 7 September 1740, O¹ 385, fol. 340, AN; letters from local officials in response to a circular from the royal procurator of Paris Châtelet, F¹¹ 222, AN; Narbonne, Journal, p. 483; Bricourt, et al., "La Crise de subsistance des années 1740," pp. 308-313; Foucaud to PG, 23 September 1740, Coll. JF 1121, fols. 267-268; Odile, royal procurator at Dourdan, 5 November 1740, 4B 1140, AD Seine-et-Oise. Nor, as Bricourt et al. suggest, was the 1741 harvest generally excellent. See J. M. Desbordes, ed., La Chronique villageoise de Varreddes (Paris, n.d.), pp. 25-26.

[153] The same boisseau that the Paris factor de La Roche sold for 1.4 livres in December 1737 commanded 3.6 livres years later. D5B⁶ 753 and 5655, Arch. Seine-Paris. The Paris merchant N.-L. Martin sold a setier of wheat for 14.5 livres in December 1737 and for 38 livres in December 1740. D5B⁶ 3118, Arch. Seine-Paris. Prices were even higher in the hinterland. See J. Dupâquier, M. Lachiver, and J. Meuvret, Mercuriales du pays de France et du Vexin français (1640-1792) (Paris, 1968), pp. 169-175. For quarterly Paris prices see M. Baulant, "Le Prix des grains à Paris de 1431 à 1788," Annales: économies, sociétés, civilisations, 23rd year (May-June 1968): 520-540.

[154] See Gazetins de police, 11-12 October 1740, MS. Bast. 10167, fol. 156; Mémoires de Luynes, 3: 255 (25 September 1740); deliberations of bureau of Hôtel de Ville, 5 February 1741, H 1859,

to burgeoning unemployment, proliferating mendicancy, and what several commentators called "universal misery."[155] The winters of 1739–1740 and 1740–1741 were "violently" bitter and the Seine inundated the capital during the Christmas season of 1740.[156] Strained to the breaking point by a relentless influx of the sick and miserable, the Hôtel-Dieu warned of further calamities as a result of dearth-linked *maladies populaires.*[157] While the women of the faubourg St.-Marcel "talked of nothing but dying of hunger," reports of soaring mortality poured in from the countryside.[158]

Given these conditions, the famine plot syndrome quickly developed. Many of its features will seem familiar to us. As in 1725, there was a general refusal to believe that the scarcity was "real." It was a "phony dearth" caused by "the malice of men" rather than by bad weather (the police reported Parisians to believe)—a conviction that was shared by a number of local officials in the hinterland.[159] Only a sinister plot, wrote one of the latter, could explain the cruel paradox that has us "dying of hunger in the midst of abundance."[160] By the fall of 1740, according to another Parisian observer, there was no longer any doubt in the minds of the people "that the ministry is engaged in manipulations of the grain supply."[161]

The evidence adduced in support of this contention was remarkably

---

fols. 204–207, AN. This despite the "taxation" policy followed by the police. See, for example, 4 March 1739, Y 12141, AN; Gazetins, 26 May 1740 and 14 April 1741, MS. Bast. 10167, fol. 118 and 10168, fol. 168; 9 July 1740, Y 13747 and 2 September 1740, Y 9441, AN. See the similar experience at Corbeil. "Journal d'un bourgeois de Corbeil," *Bulletin de la Société historique et archéologique de Corbeil, d'Etampes, et du Hurepoix,* 4th year (1898): p. 36.

[155] 6 May 1739, *Lettres du commissaire Dubuisson,* pp. 550–551; Assemblées de Police, 8 January, 23 April 1739, MS. fr. 11356, fols. 376, 393, BN; anon. to LG, 1740, MS. Bast., 10027, fols. 391–392; curé de Saint-Jean-en-Grève to LG, 20 April 1739, MS. Bast. 10276; curé de Saint-Jean de la Boucherie to LG, 18 May 1739, MS. Bast. 10276; Gazetins de police, 21 September 1740, MS. Bast. 10167, fol. 138; "Journal d'un bourgeois de Corbeil," p. 36; Denoyelle to PG, 21 September 1740, Coll. JF 1123, fol. 166; PG to CG, 5 December 1738, Coll. JF 1119, fol. 34; Odile to PG, 19 October 1738, Coll. JF 1119, fol. 108; Rossignol to PG, 26 November 1740, Coll. JF 1307, fols. 58–59; Gazetins, 30 May 1741, MS. 621, fol. 173, Bibliothèque Historique de la Ville de Paris (hereafter BHVP); Breteuil to LG, 29 March 1740, MS. Bast. 10321; duc de Richelieu to comte de Chatte, 24 October 1740, in A. de Boislisle, ed., *Mémoires authentiques du maréchal de Richelieu (1725–1757)* (Paris, 1918), p. 181.

[156] "Inondation de 1740," MS. fr. 5682, fol. 194, BN; *Journal de Barbier* (ed. 1858), 3: 243–244 (December 1740); W. Mildmay, *The Police of Paris* (London, 1763), p. 98; Maurepas to Marville, 12 January 1741, 3 AZ 10², pièce 2, Arch. Seine-Paris; Savart to Leduc, 10, 14, 21 January 1741, MS. Bast. 10277; livre de Conciergerie, AB, AAP; *Mercure suisse* (December 1740), 162; 30 January 1740, *Lettres du commissaire Dubuisson,* p. 613.

[157] Deliberations of bureau of Hôtel-Dieu, 7 October 1740 and 25 April 1741, nos. 109 and 110, AAP.

[158] Gazetins de police, 19–20 September 1740, MS. Bast. 10167; d'Argenson, *Journal,* ed. by Rathery, 2: 182 (10 July 1740); Mercier, *Tableau,* 1: 57; J. Delumeau, "Démographie d'un port français sous l'ancien régime: Saint-Malo (1651–1750)," *XVIIe Siècle,* 86–87: 3–21; M. Couturier, *Recherches sur les structures sociales de Châteaudun, 1525–1789* (Paris, 1969), pp. 102–106; L. Henry and C. Lévy, "Quelques données sur la région autour de Paris au 18e siècle," *Population,* 17th year (April–June 1962): 306–307; Bricourt *et al.,* "La Crise de subsistance des années 1740," pp. 289–291, 324–333.

[159] Gazetins de police, 10, 11 January, 28–29 September, 16–17 October 1740, 28 February 1741, MS. Bast. 10167, fols. 7, 147, 159 and 10168, fol. 54; Guillemin to PG, 19 September 1740, Coll. JF 1123, fol. 168; Garnier to PG, 22 August 1740, Coll. JF 1123, fol. 261.

[160] Guillemin to PG, 18 September 1740, Coll. JF 1123, fol. 166.

[161] Gazetins de police, 16 September 1740, MS. Bast. 10167, fols. 132–133.

similar to that cited in 1725–1726. It was charged that the government prohibited grain holders in the countryside from selling to anyone but "emissaries of the *partisans*" and forbade *laboureurs* from offering their grain in the public markets until the Company of the Indies had sold all of its grain, some of which was repurchased by its own agents in order to sustain high prices.[162] A variation on this accusation had it that *laboureurs* were barred "because there are rotten government stocks that had to be sold."[163] While the evidence shows that the *laboureurs* were obliged not to keep away from the markets but to furnish them regularly, it is again quite likely that the authorities gave priority to the sale of the king's grain.[164]

As for quality, complaints were less strident in 1740 than in 1725, perhaps because the controller-general, Orry, was acutely sensitive to the problem of grain conservation. He demanded that grain purchased in the king's name for Paris be of excellent quality and arranged for grain of "bad or altered quality" to be reconditioned and sold in the provinces.[165] The Assembly of Police was reluctant to accept army grain for the capital because it was often "not of good quality."[166] The leading individual Paris victualer of 1740, Thellusson, also insisted on "irreproachable" quality in his purchases.[167] Still, a certain amount of grain was spoiled because of inadequate storage facilities in the capital.[168] On occasion, irremediably spoiled grain was thrown in the river, but, predictably, the act was interpreted as proof of "vile maneuvers" rather than as a measure of public hygiene.[169] Complaints about bread quality appeared to be the result of the inability of the Paris bakers to work the very hard Mediterranean wheat, despite training from Provençal specialists.[170]

As in 1725, there was deep suspicion that the so-called foreign grain was no less phony than the dearth itself, that it was domestic grain cached abroad and then imported with an exotic label.[171] This charge was given

---

[162] Ibid., 10, 11 January, 18, 19 October, 11, 12 December 1740, 28, 29 April, 26, 27 May 1741, MS. Bast. 10167, fols. 7, 161, 193 and 10168, fols. 181, 246.

[163] Unknown to LG, MS. Bast. 10027, fol. 391.

[164] As in 1725, the government virtually requisitioned *laboureur* grain by imposing weekly quotas through the lieutenant of police of Paris and the intendants of the surrounding generalities. See Coll. JF 1121, fols. 148–149 and Narbonne, *Journal*, pp. 470–473.

[165] CG to Buron, 31 October 1740, 10 January 1741, KK 1005F, AN; CG to Buron, 28 June, 23 July 1741, G⁷ 58, AN; CG to Artaud, 13 March, 19 April 1741, KK 1005F; CG to Pallu, 29 December 1740, 19 April 1741, KK 1005F. But Orry was not always successful. See, for example, BN, Coll. JF 1120, fols., 7, 8. It is clear both from police reports and from the registers of merchant-factors that the Paris bakers tried to buy as little foreign grain as possible. See the August 1740 entries in N. L. Martin's sales registers. D5B⁶ 3118, Arch. Seine-Paris, and Assemblée de Police, 8 January 1739, MS. fr. 11356, fols. 375–76, BN.

[166] Assemblée de Police, 4 December 1738, MS. fr. 11356, fol. 370, BN.

[167] Thellusson to PG, 1 July 1741, Coll. JF 1109, fols. 124–125. Cf. Lüthy, *Banque*, 2: 198.

[168] Thellusson to LG, 10 January, 7 February, 4, 18 April 1739, MS. Bast. 10276; Coll. JF 1120, fols. 5, 6; Breteuil to LG, 28 December 1740, MS. Bast. 10277.

[169] Thellusson, *état*, March 1741, Coll. JF 1109, fols. 109–110.

[170] Béguillet, *Traité des subsistances*, p. 707n. Certain Parisians were quoted as believing that the grain that was used to bake bread for the poor in specially constructed royal ovens was "rotten" and predicted that it would "cause several diseases." Gazetins de police, 16 January 1741, MS. Bast. 10168, fol. 6.

[171] Gazetins de police, 28, 29 September 1740, MS. Bast., 10167, fol. 147.

credibility by another that was indeed true in part. Because the thirties were years of relative subsistence ease, the government permitted very high levels of grain exports. These exports continued at least until the end of 1738 when the Assembly of Police, on Hérault's motion, asked the controller-general to embargo grain and when Hérault asked him for authorization to repurchase three boatloads of grain bound for Portugal.[172] Now there were few old-regime issues more delicate and more combustible than grain export policy. As a rule such exports were prohibited, save in exceptional circumstances and with special permission, and illicit exportation was in principle still punishable by death. The grain exporter was reviled as the most vicious of merchants, for he was prepared to sell out his compatriots for a price.[173] Once the dearth began, in retrospect the government's liberal export stand seemed at best negligent and at worst culpable. The police commissaire Dubuisson deplored the government's open door policy because it destroyed the nation's ability to resist a shortage; he agreed with other contemporaries that this lack of foresight was "a defect in government."[174]

D'Argenson found more than imprudence to denounce: Orry and his brother profited immensely from the export licenses they sold without regard for the "misery" and the "famine" they caused.[175] Such charges from the pen of an enemy might be discounted if they were not voiced in many other quarters as well. As late as the fall of 1740 Orry was said to be authorizing exports for Austria and for Spain (at whose court his father had once occupied a high post).[176] And given the flawed grasp of royal centralization, exportation continued in a number of places even after the ministry suspended it.[177]

As in 1725, there were other factors that gave a certain verisimilitude to the plot apprehensions. There were "secret storehouses" of grain set up "on the orders of the court" throughout the realm, it was alleged.[178] One such criminal outpost, wrote the marquis d'Argenson, was located near the

---

[172] Assemblée de Police, 3 July, mid-November 1738, ms. fr. 11356, fols. 345, 367-69, BN; LG to CG, 16 November 1738, ms. Bast. 10275. On the tolerance for exportation in the thirties, see Coll. JF 1314, fol. 135.

[173] On traditional policies and attitudes regarding exports, see Kaplan, *Bread, Politics and Political Economy*, especially vol. 1.

[174] 6 May 1739, *Lettres du commissaire Dubuisson*, p. 550; gazetins de police, 18, 19 October 1740, ms. Bast. 10167, fol. 161. The leading victualers of the 1770s and '80s, the Leleu brothers, agreed with this assessment. "Observations par les sieurs Leleu au principal ministre," 14 August 1788, p. 14. Turgot in 1775, like Orry in 1740, was accused of "giving up our grain to the foreigner." Michelet, *Histoire de France*, 16: 196.

[175] D'Argenson, *Journal*, ed. by Rathery, 3: 84, 183 (28 May, 29 September 1740).

[176] Gazetins de police, 23, 24 September, 18, 19 October 1740, ms. Bast. 10167, fols. 140, 161; d'Argenson, *Journal*, ed. by Rathery, 3: 84 (28 May 1740). On Orry's father's Spanish connections, see *Mémoires de Maurepas*, 2: 186–189 and L.-E.-A. Jobez, *La France sous Louis XV* (Paris, 1864–1873), 2: 513.

[177] French opinion on illegal or immoral grain exportation was not very much different from the conviction of many Californians during the period of burgeoning shortages in the spring of 1979 that American companies were selling their precious gasoline to Mexico. *Newsweek*, 21 May 1979.

[178] Gazetins de police, 16, 17 October 1740, ms. Bast. 10167, fol. 159.

canal d'Orléans.[179] In fact, the Briare-Orléans canal system was the primary provisioning route used by the government to ship emergency supplies from the Mediterranean and the Lyonnais to the capital and there were numerous storage depots along its path.[180] Suspicions were also aroused by competitive buying (occasionally marked by reckless bidding or other indiscretions) by representatives of different and sometimes rival jurisdictions and institutions—though it should be added that Orry gradually succeeded in imposing a certain degree of coordination on both purchasing and distribution.[181] The news that the ministry rebuffed the propositions of several civic-minded merchants to help provision the capital seemed to be further evidence of conspiracy.[182]

Again in 1740 the ministry fomented doubts about its motives as a result of its pricing policy. Once the king's grain became involved, consumers tended to believe *si veut le Roi, si veut la mercuriale*. Since prices did not fall rapidly after government grain began to reach the markets in large amounts, then in the harsh logic of the frightened consumer, it followed that "it is the ministry itself that is the cause of high prices."[183] D'Argenson understood government policy very well (though elsewhere he took a much less generous view of the motives of the leaders):

Can one imagine that the government wishes to profit from such distress? No, but it is public avarice that is the cause of such operations. The ministry fears that it will cost too much for the grain that it imports from abroad, and it has thus resolved to keep bread at 5 sous throughout the realm until the next harvest. . . .[184]

Narbonne noticed the same phenomenon: Orry kept the prices on king's grain surprisingly high because he "did not want the king to take a loss."[185] In letter after letter to his subordinates, the controller-general insisted that government grain must be sold at no less than 20 or 25 sous below the going market price. Local officials who ceded to consumer pressures and sold their allotments at a signficantly lower price received stern reprimands and had their supplies cut off.

While Orry had staked his reputation from the beginning of his ministry on reducing the budget deficit, economy was not the only reason for his

---

[179] D'Argenson, *Journal*, ed. by Rathery, 3: 222 (14 November 1740).

[180] CG to Buron, 11 December 1740 and CG to Jomarron, 26 May 1741, KK 1005F, AN; CG to Buron, 23 July 1741, G⁷ 58, AN; CG to PG, 21 September 1740 and *états des magasins*, Coll. JF 1121, fols. 97, 259. On the canal system, see: J. Expilly, *Dictionnaire géographique, historique et politique des Gaules et de la France* (Paris, 1762), 1: 849; Couet de Montbayeux to PG, 9 October 1725, MS. Bast. 10270, pièces 211–214; "Mémoire de la généralité de Paris," MS. fr. 32595, fols. 10, 11, BN.

[181] See CG to LG, 23 September 1740 and LG to PG, 12 October 1740, Coll. JF 1121, fols. 100, 205; CG to Artaud, 13 March 1741, KK 1005F, AN; Tastevin to LG, 20 July 1740, MS. Bast. 10277.

[182] Gazetins de police, 16, 17 October 1740, MS. Bast. 10167, fol. 160. Orry apparently rejected the proposition of a former associate of Samuel Bernard. D'Argenson, *Journal*, ed. by Rathery, 3: 132 (10 July 1740).

[183] Gazetins de police, 21, 22 October 1740, MS. Bast. 10167, fol. 165.

[184] D'Argenson, *Journal*, ed. by Rathery, 3: 215–216 (6 November 1740).

[185] Narbonne, *Journal*, pp. 484–485. See Barbier's similar observations at a later date. *Journal de Barbier* (ed. 1858), 3: 276 (April 1741).

tight-fisted policy. Low prices, Orry believed, might produce instant consumer gratification, but only at the cost of further disrupting the market.
Stable conditions could only be restored by canalizing market forces rather
than trying to overwhelm them. Instead of using the king's grain to blud-
geon the market, Orry hoped that the market price, in response to gentle
prodding, "would fall on its own, thus lowering the price of the king's
grain in proportion." For if the downward trend did not appear to be
genuinely irreversible and if local dealers did not therefore "open their
granaries," as soon as the dose of king's grain was depleted, prices would
again soar.[186] This conservative strategy was warmly endorsed by Parisian
authorities. "We concluded," read the minutes of the Assembly of Police,
"that whenever the king supplies grain we must never allow it to be sold
more than a few sous below the market price for fear of seeing individual
dealers cut off their supply, bakers buy up everything in one fell swoop,
our financial resources exhausted, the price promptly return to high levels
afterward, and the merchants return to profit from these disasters."[187]

It is easy to imagine what frustration and confusion this policy created
for consumers. For them the king's grain was supposed to be manna, a
panacea, and not a tactical field weapon. They could not reconcile news of
huge grain arrivals with relatively piddling price adjustments. Ineluctably,
government manipulation became suspect. Moreover, had they been privy
to it, what would these consumers have made of Thellusson's boast—meant
as testimony to his managerial prowess—that he "made money for the
king"?[188] What better confirmation of the existence of a plot?

In 1740, as in 1725, the people warned that they would not tolerate the
dearth-exploitation much longer and observers of the people described
them as teetering on the brink of revolt. In the fall of 1740 a rambling,
roughcast letter-tract signed "Meur de Fint" [Dying of Hunger] warned
Lieutenant General Marville that "we are 20,000 strong" ready to burn the
capital in the name of "all the miserable of Paris" if he did not lower the
price of bread within the month.[189] Two years before, on the same grounds,
a poster threatened the burning of the house of Marville's predecessor,
Hérault, who had been something of a popular hero in 1725–1726.[190] In

---

[186] CG to Buron, 10, 30 June 1741 and CG to Belamy, 1741, G⁷ 58, AN. Cf. CG to PG, 17
September 1740, Coll. JF 1121, fol. 76 and Savart to Leduc, January 1741, MS. Bast. 10277.

[187] Assemblée de Police, 22 January 1739, MS. fr. 11356, fols. 379–380, BN. See 19 May 1740,
ibid., fols. 413–414.

[188] Thellusson to PG, 1 July 1741, Coll. JF 1109, fols. 124–25. Thellusson meant that, globally,
he sold royal grain for more than he paid for it, not counting losses at sea and other aberrations.
See also M. L'Héritier, L'Intendant Tourny (1695–1760) (Paris, 1920), 1: 388.

[189] October 1740, MS. Bast. 10277. Though there were some doubts about Marville's com-
petence and especially about his ability to stand up to the ministry, on balance he seems to
have been viewed favorably by the public. See Gazetins de police, 14, 15 September, 17, 18
October 1740, 29, 30 January, 21–22 April, 9, 10 May 1741, MS. Bast. 10167, fols. 130–31, 162
and 10168, fols. 45, 174, 227.

[190] 24 October 1738, MS. Bast. 10275. The price rise of 1738 was Hérault's way of "making
the public pay his daughter's dowry," according to another mauvais discours. September 1738,
Lettres du commissaire Dubuisson, p. 49. Yet by 1740 the dominant note was nostalgia for Hérault,
who had been replaced by Marville (his daughter's husband!). "We lost everything in losing

October 1740 placards were allegedly posted on the house of the controller-general and the office of the Indies Company charging Orry with making a "million a week" on grain dealings and warning that he would be killed and his house burned "if this minister continues to make us eat such expensive bread."[191]

In late September Cardinal Fleury's carriage, passing near the Place Maubert market, was accosted by a "multitude of people shouting that they were dying of hunger and demanding cheaper bread." Nervously Fleury tried to calm them with alms and promises that prices would shortly go down.[192] Traversing Paris at about the same time, the king was similarly jarred when crowds shouted "Misery! Famine! Give us bread!" instead of the reassuring "Long live the king."[193] Even as d'Argenson reflected that "everything is ripe for revolt," so a bloody riot broke out in the Bicêtre prison as a result of a reduction in the inmates' bread ration along with a deterioration of its quality.[194] A few days later the police arrested a woman at the Maubert market for urging the crowd "to rise in revolt against the bakers."[195] A month later again at Maubert people identified as day workers angrily vowed that their patience was exhausted and that they would soon take things into their own hands.[196] If the price of bread does not decrease soon, a police agent predicted, "there is no doubt that we will see some sort of rising in Paris, for the people are already saying openly that they have only one life to lose, but before dying they will punish others with death."[197] In November a small bread riot occurred in the faubourg St.-Antoine and a "seditious spirit" continued to characterize Maubert through the beginning of 1741.[198]

In 1740, as in 1725, stories circulated that Good Samaritans at the court were trying to speak the truth about the dearth in the highest councils of the realm. The leading figure in most of these was the late regent's son, the duc d'Orléans, and they fit nicely in the Orléanist political tradition. Orléans was depicted as boldly informing Louis XV that "the public of Paris is saying out loud that it is Your Majesty who runs the grain trade, or if not you then the Company of the Indies on your orders or M. Orry

---

Hérault," Parisians were reported as lamenting. Hérault was portrayed as a man with influence in the royal council who dared to stand up for the public interest. Gazetins de police, 19, 20, 25, 26, 28, 29 Sept. 1740, MS. Bast. 10167, fols. 137, 144, 147–148.

[191] Gazetins de police, 26, 27 October 1740, MS. Bast. 10167, fol. 167.

[192] 23, 24, 28, 29 September 1740, ibid., fols. 141, 148; Journal de Barbier (ed. 1858), 3: 219–220 (September 1740); Mercure historique et politique, 109 (October 1740): 476.

[193] Gazetins de police, 19, 20 September 1740, MS. Bast. 10167, fol. 136; d'Argenson, Journal, ed. by Rathery, 3: 172 (24 September 1740). Cf. Narbonne, Journal, p. 468.

[194] D'Argenson, Journal, ed. by Rathery, 3: 171 (23 September 1740); LG to PG, 22 September 1740, Coll. JF 1140, fol. 53; Mémoires de Luynes, 3: 255 (September 1740); Journal de Barbier (ed. 1858), 3: 219 (September 1740).

[195] LG to PG, 28 September 1740, Coll. JF 1121, fol. 110.

[196] Gazetins de police, 21, 22 October 1740, MS. Bast. 10167, fol. 166. There were similar risings at Bicêtre and the Salpêtrière in 1771 and at the Salpêtrière again in 1773. Hardy's Journal, 1 February 1771, MS. fr. 6680, BN and Sartine to Guyot, 8 May 1773, Y 13551, AN.

[197] Gazetins de police, 16, 17 October 1740, MS. Bast. 10167, fol. 159.

[198] 8, 9 November, 22, 24 December 1740, ibid., fols. 174, 199.

by abuse of his authority." "Unless the government changed its system of dealing with grain," he admonished, the king would "alienate the hearts of all his subjects." Orléans was said to have vividly described the suffering of the people in the provinces and the "extreme misery" to which "a third of the people of Paris" were reduced. He exhorted Louis to take action for their sake and to salvage the royal reputation. He proposed an investigation of recent exports, a prohibition against "pillaging" by the representatives of the Indies Company, and a lowering of the price of the king's grain.[199]

In 1725 denunciations such as these appeared to have led to the overthrow of Bourbon's cabal. It may have been memories of that episode that prompted these scenarios of wishful thinking in 1740. But it must have been disquieting to recall that the hero-martyr of 1725–1726, Cardinal Fleury, was now known to be on the side of evil.[200]

Saint-Simon and many far humbler and less articulate Parisians frankly likened Fleury's "grain maneuvers" to those of the duc de Bourbon in 1725.[201] It proved more difficult, however, to make the case against the cardinal than it had been to make it against the duke because, at least until now, there was very little reproach to visit on Fleury in either his public or private life. The case against the cardinal was composed of fragments of accusations that did not fit together in a convincing whole but were corrosive enough to discredit him. He was vulnerable, and he was placed at the center of the conspiracy, simply because he was the senior minister— "rather an absolute king than a prime minister," wrote Saint-Simon, reflecting a widely held view of Fleury's influence—and as such he was presumed to be responsible for what transpired both in the government and in the nation.[202]

All the charges were serious, but they carried different burdens of obloquy. The most infamous, which were also the most out of character, portrayed Fleury as an "odious" and "tyrannical" schemer, "naturally callous about the people's well-being," who organized the famine and the "monopoly" on supply by arranging "excessive exports" and "massive removals of grain" from the interior.[203] He transformed provisioning into

---

[199] 16, 17, 18, 21, 22, 26 September 1740, ibid., fols. 132–33, 134, 139, 145. D'Argenson reported that Orléans dramatically handed the king a vile loaf of fern bread in the midst of a meeting of the royal council to underline the misery of consumers. *Journal*, ed. by Rathery, 2: 27 (19 May 1739). It is interesting to note that d'Argenson, one of the most virulent critics of the Fleury-Orry ministry, was closely connected with the Orléans family. *Journal de Barbier* (ed. 1866), 3: 239 and d'Argenson, *Journal*, ed. by Rathery, 3: 165 ff. (September 1740). The duc de La Rochefoucauld and several bishops also candidly spoke to Louis XV about the extreme misery of the people. D'Argenson, *Journal*, ed. by d'Argenson, 2: 26–28, 34. The Parisian municipality evoked the suffering of the people in its harangue to the king, but in very reserved terms. *Mémoires de Luynes*, 3: 219 (August 1740).

[200] According to one report Orléans became persona non grata at the court because he denounced Fleury, in the king's presence, "as the sole cause of the misery that afflicts this kingdom." Gazetins de police, 13, 14 October 1740, MS. Bast. 10167, fol. 158.

[201] 14, 15, 23, 24 September 1740, ibid., fols. 130–31, 141; *Mémoires de Saint-Simon*, 20: 203.

[202] *Mémoires de Saint-Simon*, 6: 52. Cf. ibid., 36: 215.

[203] Gazetins de police, 14, 15, 17, 18 September, 13, 14 October 1740 and 3, 4 January, 30 March, 7, 8 April 1741, MS. Bast. 10167, fols. 130–31, 134, 158 and 10168, fols. 34, 100, 155.

"a dreadful traffic" either in order to satisfy his own avidity (yet this must have seemed preposterous given this octogenarian's relatively ascetic life) or to enrich his family in anticipation of his not-too-distant demise or to reward certain "seigneurs" possessed of "a mercenary soul" such as the Orrys and the maréchal de Noailles.[204] The least opprobrious motive imputed to the cardinal was "avarice for the State" rather than in behalf of himself or his protégés: dear bread as a fiscal expedient to procure "money without imposing further taxes" in order to meet a 40,000,000 livres deficit swelled by onerous military and naval expenses that had not been foreseen.[205] Fleury was said to be mortified when he heard the epigram comparing the way in which the three cardinal-physicians administered the body politic: Richelieu "bled" by cutting off heads, Mazarin "purged" by extorting money, and Fleury prescribed "a diet because of the bread scarcity."[206]

In fact, Doctor Fleury left the care of the kingdom to others, prescribing for himself nothing more reinvigorating than public prayers.[207] D'Argenson, who hated Fleury, blamed him for allowing "the dearth to gain ground" by having procrastinated when it was imperative to act because he did not want to spend limited royal funds on emergency grain supplies.[208] But if it is true that the ministry waited too long before engaging itself massively on the supply side (this question remains open to debate) it was not directly Fleury's fault. Right after the harvest of 1738, Fleury expressed great concern for the shortage, but he clearly counted on the controller-general and the Parisian Assembly of Police to elaborate a policy for parrying it.[209] Recurrent illness during much of 1739–1740 reinforced Fleury's dependence upon Orry, in whom he invested great confidence—for good reasons.[210]

D'Argenson cruelly mocked the cardinal for confessing, in frustration, when asked to account for the continued rise in the bread price in the fall of 1740, that "he just didn't understand anything anymore."[211] Yet it is quite likely that Fleury blurted out the truth, that the situation was not merely

---

According to one report, Fleury's advisers persuaded him that the stories of popular suffering were not worthy of attention because they were merely "tales spread by the Chauvelin party meant to discredit his ministry." D'Argenson, *Journal*, ed. by d'Argenson, 2: 25.

[204] Gazetins de police, 28, 29 September, 1, 2, 18, 19 October, 23, 24 November 1740, MS. Bast. 10167, fols. 147, 151, 161, 179–80; Raunié, *Chansonnier historique*, 6: 263. There was one incident that gives a certain credence to the accusations of "family" rapacity. In defiance of the lieutenant general's orders to sell its English grain at the current market price in June 1740, a provisioning "company" led by Fleury's brother-in-law tried to sell at 3 livres above that standard. Marville may have protested directly to the cardinal. Assemblée de Police, 30 June 1740, MS. fr. 11356, fol. 419, BN.

[205] *Mémoires de Saint-Simon*, 34: 314–315; Gazetins de police, 16, 17 October, 23, 24 November 1740, MS. Bast. 10167, fols. 160, 179.

[206] *Journal de Barbier* (ed. 1858), 3: 240 (December 1740); d'Argenson, *Journal*, ed. by d'Argenson, 2: 34 (November 1740).

[207] 9 May 1739, Coll. JF 1120, fol. 22; Kaplan, "The Uses of Saint Geneviève."

[208] D'Argenson, *Journal*, ed. by d'Argenson, 2: 117 (5 December 1739). See also ibid., 2: 92 (5 July 1739).

[209] 20 October 1738, Coll. JF 1119, fol. 9.

[210] Jobez, *Louis XV*, 3: 174.

[211] D'Argenson, *Journal*, ed. by Rathery, 3: 196 (15 October 1740).

beyond his control but also beyond his comprehension. In response to a letter from the procurator general evoking the gravity of the crisis in September 1740, Fleury avowed "that I can do nothing from my position, I am counting entirely on you and the controller-general as well as on the prévôt des marchands and Monsieur Marville." The only thing he could think of doing was "importuning the king to reduce as much as possible his expenses," a pious and hackneyed wish that was ludicrously remote from the task at hand. Trying to be useful, Fleury mentioned in his letter that the prince of Lichtenstein had told him the day before that there was grain in quite large concentrations about sixty kilometers from Paris, "but he did not know in what place."[212] Such extravagant ingenuousness in the face of a crisis could not have been feigned. The cardinal was too impotent to take an active part in any conspiracy.

In one of the plot scenarios least unfavorable to Fleury, the cardinal was said to be "unaware of the grain maneuvers" launched by Orry.[213] The controller-general was indeed much better suited to play the role of principal villain. He had become manifestly wealthier since becoming finance minister, he had a mistress who hosted illegal gambling parties where fortunes were lost and won, he had a profligate brother, he had a rough and nasty disposition, and, in any case, as the incarnation of the public treasury, he was a priori suspect.[214] At best Orry was assailed for incompetence in dealing with the dearth or for exploiting it in order to redress the government's precarious financial situation.[215] At worst, and more commonly, he was denounced for corruption. Barbier pointed to "malversations on the grain provisions"; d'Argenson inveighed against "the horrible depredations," "the unpunished hoards of grain," and "the monopoly, like an open *gabelle* on bread;" while ordinary Parisians, according to the public opinion reports, raged against "the apparent dearth fabricated by the controller-general," the "dizzying speculations" directed by Orry, and "the sordid treasure he amasses at our expense."[216]

---

[212] Fleury to PG, 19 September 1740, Coll. JF 1121, fols. 81–82. "May God enlighten you and aid us, though we hardly merit it," the cardinal concluded.

[213] Gazetins de police, 3, 4 January 1741, MS. Bast. 10168, fol. 34. Another police report mentioned the rumor that Fleury had sharply castigated Orry for improper grain management. 26, 27 September 1740, ibid., 10167, fol. 146. According to Barbier, Fleury tried to get the king to become concerned about the crisis, but Louis XV would not listen. *Journal de Barbier* (ed. 1866), 3: 219 (September 1740).

[214] Already in 1737, well before any intimation of subsistence crisis, Orry was accused of "malversation" and "negligence." *Mémoires de Luynes*, 1: 371 (October 1737); 20 November 1737, *Lettres du commissaire Dubuisson*, pp. 399–400. Barbier claimed that Orry was "generally despised." *Journal* (ed. 1858), 3: 240 (December 1740). See the similar vilification of Terray, another controller-general who had a ruthless style and reformist inclinations. See Kaplan, *Bread, Politics, and Political Economy*, 2: chap. 13.

[215] D'Argenson, *Journal*, ed. by d'Argenson, 2: 195 (6 November 1740); *Journal de Barbier* (ed. 1858), 3: 236 (November 1740).

[216] *Journal de Barbier* (ed. 1858), 3: 240 (December 1740); d'Argenson, *Journal*, ed. by Rathery, 3: 170–71, 219, 224 (23 September, 8, 14 November 1740); Gazetins de police, 17, 26, 27 September, 1, 2, 26 October 1740, MS. Bast. 10167, fols. 134, 145, 149, 167. Le Camus, first president of the Cour des Aides in Paris, was quoted as saying that soon Orry would be tried "by order of the king for having been the primary author of the dearth. . . ." 30 April 1720, ibid., fol. 94.

More than any other single factor, it was the conduct of Orry's brother that irretrievably compromised the controller-general. His brother, Orry de Fulvy, was an intendant of finance with whom he worked closely.[217] Highly esteemed as a brilliant administrator, Fulvy was no less reputed for leading a dissolute life. Known to have had a modest income when he began government service, Fulvy lavished immense sums on country houses, magnificent carriages, sumptuous dinners, his wife's wardrobe and jewelry, and more or less low-born mistresses. But his chief vice was gambling, an activity considered particularly unbecoming a high government official whose specialty was financial affairs. One evening in February 1739, at his brother's mistress's home, Fulvy managed to lose 480,000 livres at cards while his wife, according to some reports, lost another 240,000 without his help. It was alleged that Fulvy paid off the bulk of the debt the very next morning.[218]

This episode provoked a scandal not merely at court, where the damages could have been limited, but in the streets and marketplaces as well where the *chronique scandaleuse* was not treated with the contempt reserved for it by certain sophisticated modern historians. Even d'Argenson, who lost no occasion to revile the Orry clan, conceded that the charges against them were "perhaps very much exaggerated," but he was struck by "the rage with which the public seizes upon these rumors."[219] Fulvy's adventure was perceived as confirmation of the corruption of the Orry family. The connection with the "phony dearth" was clear in their minds: "M. Orry de Fulvy needs a way to earn back the immense sums of money that he lost at gambling." People talked of burning Fulvy's house. His wife was booed at the opera as she descended from her "flour box."[220] Had the controller-general peremptorily dismissed his brother, he might have been able to stifle the outcry and refurbish his own image. Though observers close to the court reported that Orry was furious with Fulvy for his indiscretions and that Fleury was likely to rid the government of them, the brothers remained in office and the plot allegations continued to flourish.[221]

The charges against Fulvy seemed all the more plausible because he was a director of the Company of the Indies, veteran scapegoat of the famine plot of 1725-1726. His brother, too, was closely associated with the Company whose standing he tried to repair after his predecessor as controller-general was dismissed for having embezzled Indies' funds.[222] According to one story, Fulvy obtained 500,000 livres to pay part of his gambling debts from

---

[217] *Almanach royal* (1740), 110, 119, 123, 124.

[218] H. Bonhomme, ed., *Journal et mémoires de Charles Collé* (Paris, 1968), 1: 314 (May 1751); *Mémoires de Luynes*, 2: 388-389, 392-393 (March 1739); *Journal de Barbier* (ed. 1866), 3: 159 (February 1739); 5 April 1739, *Lettres du comissaire Dubuisson*, p. 535.

[219] D'Argenson, *Journal*, ed. by Rathery, 2: 84, 89 (25, 28 February 1739).

[220] Gazetins de police, 21, 22, September, 24 December 1740, MS. Bast. 10167, fols. 138, 198.

[221] Fulvy remained an intendant of finances till his death in 1751. *Almanach royal* (1751), pp. 125, 137, 138. Just before Fulvy's demise, d'Argenson again reproached him for exposing France to "the risk of famine" by failing to organize a public provisioning campaign. *Journal*, ed. by Rathery, 6: 404 (1 May 1751).

[222] *Journal de Collé*, 1: 314 (May 1751); Lüthy, *Banque*, 2: 186-188.

the Protestant banker Vincent-Pierre Fromaget, another director of the Indies Company, who purloined it from the Company's treasury.[223] One of
the refrains of the police reports of 1739–1740 was that "the Indies Company, supported by the controller-general and M. Orry de Fulvy, is the
cause of the dearth." The directors were "insatiable persons who don't give
a damn at what price they acquire their wealth." News, which proved to
be spurious, of the arrest of a director in December 1740 elicited a joyful
response from Parisians. Like the farmers-general, the Indies directors (who
were sometimes called *partisans*) were said to have a lease from the government for the exercise of the grain monopoly. As a result "the people
will be miserable at least until 1744." The "maneuvers" of the Company
remind us of its "manipulations" fifteen years earlier: scouring the interior
to concentrate all supplies in hoards, exclusion of independent traders and
laboureurs, simulated imports, clandestine arrangements with bakers to sustain high prices, and the sale of rotten wheat. For such "odious practices,"
a police agent wrote, the people demand that the monopolists be "drawn
by four horses."[224]

In fact, Orry did not call upon the Indies Company to participate in his
mammoth provisioning campaign as had Dodun in 1725-1726.[225] With very
few exceptions he relied upon new and relatively little known men to
conduct the buying business.[226] This may explain in part Barbier's reproach
that the controller-general's operations were inefficient and costly because
he failed to consult the leading victualing specialists.[227] It is true that Orry
avoided the best known court bankers, the Bernard Circle, and the Pâris
brothers (whose resurgence in the early forties led directly to Orry's fall).
Yet he was an experienced administrator, he had good connections, and
he quickly built a small but solid organization, composed of public officials,
often of a minor level and highly motivated to perform well, of merchants
and bankers, and of amphibians straddling the nebulous frontier between
the public and private sectors.[228]

---

[223] Lüthy, *Banque*, 1: 299, 300, 415, 417n and 2: 195, 304n. The problem with this account is
that Fromaget was jailed for embezzlement in September 1738, prior to Fulvy's memorable
night, and released in June 1739. F. Funck-Brentano, *Les Lettres de cachet à Paris* (Paris, 1903),
pp. 196, 271. He had briefly been *embastillé* in 1720.

[224] Gazetins de police, 17, 21, 23, 24 September, 19, 20 October, 8, 9 November, 14 December
1740, 29 September 1741, MS. Bast. 10167, fols. 134, 137, 138, 144, 161, 164, 174, 195 and 10168,
fol. 333.

[225] Nevertheless there is some evidence that the Company imported English grain for use
in Brittany in 1738, and it appears to have done some flour importing in the forties, though
the records are extremely sketchy. Letaconnoux, *Les Subsistances en Bretagne*, p. 167 and MS.
Bast. 12405. An invoice for 500 quarters of English grain purchased in the king's name can
be found in the accounts of the Indies Company's Lorient office, but this might very well be
the result of the Company's filing error. MS. Bast. 12423, pièce 55.

[226] One of the few 1725 veterans was Tellès, a victualer closely linked to the Pâris brothers.
CG to de la Bourdonnaye, 3, 11 February 1741, KK 1005F, AN and LG to PG, 15 September
1740, Coll. JF 1121, fol. 74.

[227] *Journal de Barbier* (ed. 1858), 3: 236 (November 1740). Could this criticism have been
inspired by the powerful victualing lobby out of resentment for its exclusion?

[228] Orry's recruitment of a subdelegate named Chamart typified his strategy of using public
officials: "When all the grain operations are completed, I will see what can be done in your

Chief of staff for domestic operations, Jacques Masson was an ex-Protestant who had been director of finances for the duchy of Lorraine where he was briefly jailed on suspicion of having embezzled several millions. Presumably Orry forgave him for his earlier associations, for he had also served as agent of the Pâris brothers during the Lorraine years.[229] Subsequently, Masson made his fortune supplying wood and ship-iron to the navy and the Company of the Indies in partnership with Jean Babaud, a prosperous *négociant*. The king's grain treasury was run by Babaud's son Pierre, who married Masson's daughter. The younger Babaud ran an international trading business, built one of the greatest industrial empires of the eighteenth century, and purchased an ennobling secretaryship of the king.[230] At Lyon Orry's agents were Michel Henry and Gabriel Jars, who replaced the wealthy and influential Genevan Jean-Robert Tronchin for reasons that are not clear. Jars may have been related to the Protestant family of Etienne Perrinet de Jars, who had been a director of the Indies Company and a farmer-general in the twenties. Jars's brother, associated with one Prost in a textile business, was in charge of the king's grain at Roanne, where foreign grain was received from Arles and Marseille and prepared for shipment via the Briare canal system to Paris.[231] The controller-general also made use of the resources of the general farm for the purpose of both advancing and transferring funds for grain purchases. This liaison gives a certain credibility to yet another rendition of the plot persuasion in which the farmers-general serve as the executors of Fleury's commands.[232]

---

favor." 24 January 1742, G⁷ 59, AN. Nor did the controller-general fail to keep his word. See the rewards proposed in CG to Jomarron, 1 May 1744, G⁷ 61; CG to Breteuil, 10 May 1742, G⁷ 59; CG to Pallu, 10 June 1743, G⁷ 60.

[229] CG to Babaud, 15 January 1741, G⁷ 58, AN; Lüthy, *Banque*, 2: 412–413.

[230] CG to Benoist, 17 July 1741 and CG to Buron, 23 July 1741, G⁷ 58, AN; CG to Buron, 7 July 1741, KK 1005F, AN; CG to Babaud, 18 January 1742, G⁷ 59. On Babaud's business activities, see 29 March 1742, étude VI, liasse 694 and 3 September 1752, XCI-887, Minutier Central, AN; P. W. Bamford, "Entrepreneurship in 17th- and 18th–Century France: Some General Conditions and a Case History," *Explorations in Economic History*, 9 (April 1957): 204–213; J. P. Courthéoux, "Les Pouvoirs économiques et sociaux dans un secteur industriel: la sidérurgie," *Revue d'histoire économique et sociale*, 38 (1960): 339. The marriage of Babaud's daughter in 1756 gives a striking idea of his wealth. T 308, AN. Another member of the family, Babaud de Guerigny, rendered banking services for government grain purchasers in 1768. November 1768, D5B⁶ 284, Arch. Seine-Paris.

[231] CG to G. Jars, 7 July 1741, G⁷ 58, AN; CG to Henry, 31 March 1742 and to Jars and Prost, 11 July 1742, G⁷ 59; Dardel, *Les Ports de Rouen et du Havre*, 503; Lüthy, *Banque*, 1: 373. On the dismissal of Tronchin, see Lüthy, *Banque*, 2: 194-202 and CG to Thellusson, 30 December 1740, KK 1005F, AN. Tronchin was the brother of François Tronchin, banking associate of Isaac Thellusson, who was Orry's major supplier of foreign grain. Relations between Thellusson and Tronchin were quite strained, but it is not clear whether Thellusson or Orry took the initiative to remove J. R. Tronchin. François Tronchin married the daughter of Fromaget, Fulvy's friend and alleged benefactor, in 1736 and he had many business activities involving the Indies Company of which Fromaget was a sometime director. Lüthy, *Banque*, 2: 186-187. The year before the Tronchin marriage, Thellusson and Fromaget signed a major business deal. 22 April 1735, IV-487, Minutier Central, AN. I have uncovered no bruit linking Thellusson and the Orrys through Fromaget—perhaps because this intricate web of associations was not well known.

[232] CG to Lallemand de Betz, 14 February 1741, KK 1005F, AN; Gazetins de police, 11-12 December 1740, MS. Bast. 10167, fol. 193.

The chief supplier of foreign grain in Orry's campaign was Isaac Thellusson, one of the foremost bankers in Paris as well as Geneva's ambassador to the French court. Thellusson's diplomatic démarches in behalf of the patrician party brought him in close and frequent touch with Fleury.[233] As a banker he also had fruitful business relations with the French government. He arranged emergency grain shipments for French troops in Monaco in 1721-1722, for which task he refused to accept any commission.[234] A decade later his banking house served as paymaster as well as victualer to the French troops in Italy.[235] Skilled in international grain speculation, he profited handsomely from the export licenses accorded by Orry in the mid-thirties.[236] It is likely that the government called upon Thellusson in the subsistence crisis beginning in 1738 not only because of his court contacts and his experience, but also because of his reputation, or rather, his utter lack of celebrity. Sober and austere albeit powerful, Thellusson was virtually unknown to the public at large. At the end of the provisioning campaign in 1741, he liked to boast that he had furnished more grain in a few years than Samuel Bernard had in his whole lifetime. But it was precisely because Thellusson did not have Bernard's notoriety that he was given the opportunity to distinguish himself as a public benefactor.

Thellusson reached around the world to locate supplies. Seconded by his cousins in Amsterdam, whose banking business he had helped launch years before, and by trusted correspondents in other commercial centers, he bought in England, Ireland, America, Holland, Hamburg, Koenigsberg, Danzig, Riga, Archangel, Sicily, Genoa, and Livorno.[237] The grain trade had few mysteries for Thellusson. He knew where to buy each type of grain at different times of the year not only as a function of price but in light of different conservation practices, seasonal weather and transportation factors, and the specific characteristics of the local soils and plants.[238] He was remarkably well informed not only about harvest and supply conditions but also about the political situation in each market-nation. Thus, in anticipation of the embargoes imposed by England and the northern countries toward the end of 1740, Thellusson was able to accelerate his purchases

---

[233] Lüthy, *Banque*, 2: 178–184; Lüthy, "Une diplomatie ornée de glaces. La Représentation de Genève à la cour de France au 18e siècle," *Bulletin de la Société d'histoire et d'archéologie de Genève* (1960), pp. 9–42.

[234] "Mémoire," 18 July 1723, G⁷ 1660-1665, AN. In the aftermath of this operation, Thellusson had a taste of the way in which the government frequently treated victualers, for his accounts were challenged and his payment was delayed. Ibid. For Thellusson's private grain business at the time, see 5 May 1722, D3B⁶ 23, Arch. Seine-Paris.

[235] Lüthy, *Banque*, 2: 191–192.

[236] It is possible that Thellusson obtained some of his export licenses through bribery. Ibid., 2: 193. Cf. export enterprises similar to those of the 1730s conducted by the successor bank Thellusson, Necker and Company in the 1750s. C 1660, AD, Ille-et-Vilaine.

[237] On his international buying network, see MS. Bast. 10275, 10276, 10279 and Coll. JF 1109. Thellusson's correspondent at Nantes was the shipper and slave-trader Gabriel Michel, whom Lüthy says was a member of "the Fromaget group." *Banque*, 2: 199 and *état*, 1 July 1741, Coll. JF 1109, fol. 128.

[238] See, for example, his discourse on rye to PG, 30 September 1740, Coll. JF 1109, fols. 27–28.

and to locate alternate sources in the Mediterranean region before the full price repercussions were felt.[239]

Thellusson believed in himself; he never doubted for a moment his ability to rescue the capital.[240] Nor did he rush the ministry or seek to inflate his mission by exaggerating the gravity of the crisis. On the contrary, lucid and prudent, he advised against precipitate action and against panic stocking or selling.[241] But he insisted upon the need for a global, coordinated strategy for each operation. Purchases must be carefully planned "and they must be made in diverse places and markets not only the same day but if possible at the same hour."[242] He had a certain disdain for the parochialism and inertia of French administration, but he was infinitely easier to deal with than had been Samuel Bernard, for he did not demand to be courted and he took orders as easily as he issued them.[243]

Despite considerable overlap, Thellusson really conducted two separate buying campaigns during the harvest-years of 1738 and 1740. Between December 1738 and June 1739 he imported at least 6,000 muids of wheat and the equivalent of another thousand muids in flour. Between October 1740 and June 1741 Thellusson bought at least 27,075 muids of wheat, 4,252 muids of rye and 1,383 muids of barley. In addition to this stock of king's grain, whose magnitude is surely understated in the fragmentary records that have survived, he furnished the Paris General Hospital with wheat and secondary grain and he procured hundreds of thousands of pounds of rice for the royal government, the municipality, and the public assistance institutions.[244]

Despite Thellusson's enormous presence in the capital in these years, his name is almost never cited in the scores of denunciations and rumors that filled the air in the period 1738–1741. On the few occasions when he did appear in the police reports on opinion, the public was said to distinguish between the Indies Company monopoly grain and Thellusson's provision on which "His Majesty does not intend to make any profits" or to maintain that Thellusson was responsible to Marville rather than Orry and thus outside the conspiratorial network.[245]

Thellusson was the only major victualer in the eighteenth century to walk away unscathed from his provisioning operations. He was also one of the few major victualers who was spared an inquisitorial audit by the government. Orry had been brutally frank with Bernard, despite his great

---

[239] Thellusson to PG, 5 December 1740, ibid., fols. 69–71.

[240] On his buoyant self-confidence and optimism, see Thellusson to PG, 19 September 1740 and 7 July 1741, ibid., fols. 19, 129–130.

[241] Thellusson to prévôt des marchands, 21 January 1739, MS. Bast. 10276.

[242] Thellusson to PG, 23 October 1740, Coll. JF 1109, fols. 46–47.

[243] See his impatience with the inability of officials to comprehend the international exchange system ("the sum that you have determined for England is actually twenty-three times greater than you think"). Thellusson to (?), 3 February 1739, MS. Bast. 10276. On the other hand, see his invitation to the first president and the procurator–general to share "a lovely trout just sent to me from Geneva." 23 January 1741, Coll. JF, 1109, fol. 91.

[244] For grain purchases, see primarily MS. Bast. 10275 and 10276. For rice, see F[11] 264, AN; 6 May 1739, H 1858, fols. 178–181 and 26 May 1739, H 1939[1], AN.

[245] Gazetins de police, 19, 20 September, 3, 4 November 1740, MS. Bast. 10167, fols. 136, 170.

stature, and he mercilessly hectored his provisioning agents in 1740–1741 to account for every sou spent not only on domestic grain purchases but also on wooden planks, grain sacks, brooms, and so on.[246] Yet there is no evidence that he questioned Thellusson's expenses which amounted to well over 10,000,000 livres.[247] The Genevan boasted that he conducted this public victualing enterprise with more "economy" than he ran his own business.[248] As if to underline the point and also to demonstrate that he served the public "with more disinterest than a Frenchman would [have]," he apparently renounced all commissions and even his incidental expenses for the second campaign. He asked only for money to pay his correspondents the sums due to them, which gave him ample opportunity to realize what Lüthy calls "invisible" profits on such things as currency exchange and alleged losses.[249]

But Thellusson does seem to have been primarily interested in public honors and the status they conveyed, a quest that had marked his career from the beginning. Instead of remuneration, he asked the directors of the General Hospital to "say a word" about his services in their formal deliberations and he treasured the gold medal and the public commendation he received from the city fathers and the gold snuff-box presented to him by the king.[250]

There was at least one scandal in Thellusson's undertaking which, had it become known sooner, might have provoked a government investigation and might have besmirched the banker's reputation. Ironically, it concerned just the sort of questionable practices that helped shape the famine plot persuasion. During the first provisioning campaign Thellusson and François Tronchin participated for their own profit in three speculative grain op-

---

[246] On Orry's tough stand on the accounts, see CG to G. Jars, 7 July 1741, G⁷ 58, AN; CG to Babaud, 11 July 1742, G⁷ 59; CG to G. Jars, 20 April 1743, CG to Henry, 27 April 1743, CG to Pallu, 20 October 1743, G⁷ 60; CG to Fleuriau, 17 April 1744, G⁷ 61; CG to Pallu, 19 April 1741, KK 1005F, AN.

[247] I suppose that Orry's failure to challenge Thellusson's accounts could be interpreted as evidence of their complicity in the plot. F. Tronchin later claimed that Thellusson only kept the most summary records. Lüthy, *Banque*, 2: 198. Yet Thellusson was characteristically extremely cautious, almost litigious, in his dealings with government officials. Refusing to act on orally given orders, he always demanded written instructions. Repeatedly, he offered to present his books and the accounts of his correspondents for examination. Thellusson to PG, 19, 26 September 1740, Coll. JF 1109, fols. 19, 26.

[248] Thellusson to PG, 16 October 1740, ibid., fol. 37.

[249] Thellusson to PG, 19 September 1740, 27 June 1741, ibid., fols. 19, 121–122; deliberations of bureau of Hôtel de Ville, 18 December 1739, H 1858, fols. 340–341, AN. It is possible the renunciation only concerned his purchases for the Hôpital Général and the Hôtel de Ville, but given the internal evidence this seems highly improbable. Thellusson became embroiled in a protracted squabble with his associates over victualing commissions, but this apparently concerned only the first campaign for the king's grain. Lüthy, *Banque*, 2: 197–198.

[250] Thellusson to PG, 27 June 1741, Coll. JF 1109, fols. 121–122; Arnault to PG, 29 June 1741, ibid., fol. 123; deliberations of bureau of Hôtel de Ville, 18 December 1739, H 1858, fols. 340–341, AN; Lüthy, *Banque*, 2: 201; G. Girod de l'Ain, *Les Thellusson: Histoire d'une famille du XIVe siècle à nos jours* (Neuilly-sur-Seine, 1977), pp. 53–54. The snuffbox, and another presented to him by the French government when he left his ambassadorial post, were recently sold at Sotheby's where they commanded a record price. *London Times*, 22 November 1968.

erations. Thellusson charged Tronchin with using the king's grain funds advanced by Orry to pay for his share of the private grain speculation.[251]

As a rule one should not trust the figures adduced by physiocrats on provisioning, given their violent hostility to public intervention in this domain, but I believe that Dupont's estimate that Orry spent 80,000,000 livres (including the Thellusson purchases) is not radically inflated.[252] Orry managed one of the largest victualing enterprises of the old regime. *Parti pris* aside, there is no reason to think that Orry's operation was unnecessarily expensive or inefficient, though it must be emphasized that victualing was in many ways an opaque and mysterious business.[253] Obviously it must have been enormously difficult to keep track of affairs extending from Pennsylvania to Archangel, Albania, and the Levant, and the reallocation of domestic supplies was no easy matter to control.[254] The ministry purchased grain directly through Masson and his correspondents in the provinces, but Orry also offered premiums to merchants to stimulate private initiative and authorized certain speculators to try their hand, despite his repugnance for maverick enterprises outside his immediate reach.[255] He encouraged intendants to commission both public and private buying in their jurisdictions.[256] And because provisioning was traditionally viewed

---

[251] Lüthy, *Banque*, 2: 200. Conspiracy enthusiasts will be intrigued to learn that Marville, well after he left the police, personally intervened in 1755 to arrange the confiscation of the papers of one Lebrun, "chargé des papiers et comptes pour l'achapt et la vente des bleds pour le compte du Roy en 1739, 1740, 1741." I do not know why Marville wanted these papers or what happened to them. 19 August 1755, MS. Bast. 11904.

[252] P. S. Dupont de Nemours, *Analyse historique de la législation des grains depuis 1692* (Paris, 1789), p. 33. Poussot, the police inspector specializing in subsistence affairs, estimated the amount at 25,000,000 livres, but I believe that it is too low. It is possible that he was referring just to the Paris-bound supplies or to the 1740–1741 operation. 13 May 1761, MS. Bast. 10141, fol. 480. The *Mercure suisse* set the cost of foreign grain only at 40,000,000 up to October 1740. *Mercure suisse* (October 1740): 107. Another physiocrat, Lemercier de la Rivière, wrote that Orry was left with 13,000,000 livres in grain in 1741 that he could not sell. *L'intérêt général*, p. 269. See also C. H. Piarron de Chamousset, "Observations sur la liberté," *Journal de Commerce* (September 1759): 109. It is true that Orry was left with a large stock, much of which he managed to sell in the next two years. Still, he was giving away grain by the summer of 1743. CG to Delure, 9 June 1743, G⁷ 60, AN. G. Martin estimated that the government spent 45,000,000 livres in 1709–1710 for feeding Paris and the armies. "Les Famines de 1693 et de 1709 et la spéculation sur les blés," *Bulletin du Comité des travaux historiques et scientifiques. Section des sciences économiques et sociales* (1908): 170n. For the magnitude of the operations in the sixties and seventies, see Kaplan, *Bread, Politics and Political Economy*, chaps. 8 and 13.

[253] See the report in *Journal de Barbier* (ed. 1858), 3: 236 (November 1740).

[254] On Orry's appetite for "new sources" and the Albanian project, see CG to PG, 27 September 1740, Coll. JF 1121, fol. 106.

[255] CG to PG, 19 September 1740 and PG to CG, 20 September 1740, ibid., fols. 83–84, 91–93. On individual speculative projects, see Tastevin to LG, 30 July 1740, MS. Bast. 10277 and Savart's accounts, MS. Bast. 11495. But the Parisian municipality complained that Orry did not give it a sufficiently free buying hand, especially at the outset of the crisis in 1738. *Mémoires de Luynes*, 4: 223 (September 1742) and MS. nouvelles acquisitions françaises, 1032, fol. 93, BN.

[256] CG to intendants, Coll. JF 1120, fol. 29. Of course when Orry needed to divert the intendants' supplies for Parisian consumption, he brooked no opposition. See, for example, CG to Saint-Contest, 17 October, 6 November 1740, KK 1005F, AN and CG to PG, 19 September 1740 (#2), Coll. JF 1121, fol. 83.

Victualing operations managed by intendants resulted in the emergence of local or regional plot persuasions. Thus from northern France:

as a local problem, local officials needed no encouragement to hunt for their own supplies. Still, Orry was a remarkably energetic administrator who labored to keep abreast and who took personal charge of the specific details of provisioning as well as the strategic planning wherever he could. Moreover, he managed provisioning the way one would imagine a tight-fisted finance minister running any social program. At every step he tried to cut costs, even at the risk of alienating both consumers and members of his own staff.

We do not know how Orry reacted to the plot accusations against him and the government. But we do know that he fully understood that "the spectacle of the [king's] trade in grain can upset the people and the magistrates."[257] The only policy that the controller-general had for dealing with either elite or common opinion was a negative one: to try to reduce the cues likely to trigger suspicion. He enjoined and exhorted his agents to remain as inconspicuous as possible. He urged them to buy with "as little éclat and as much expeditiousness as possible." The provenance of supplies was to be kept secret, and officials were to act unofficially as much as possible rather than by promulgating ordinances or attracting attention in other ways.[258] On numerous occasions, however, the agents and officials, for diverse reasons, did not follow these instructions. In any event, it was no easy task to try to conceal the disposition of hundreds of thousands of *setiers*. Yet even when discretion prevailed, the policy often backfired. Lack of publicity enhanced anxiety while the air of mystery and uncertainty led directly to the crystallization of suspicions.

The significance of the famine plot persuasion lies in large measure in its structural immutability, its serial sameness. Yet there was one major difference between the 1725 and 1740 experiences that merits attention. In 1725 Louis XV had remained completely on the sidelines. He had simply been too young to participate in a sordid affair. Indeed, in the minds of many people it was precisely because of the absence of a real king that the conspiracy could have occurred. By 1740, however, Louis no longer had an easy alibi. Though opinion remained divided and ambivalent, what is striking and ominous for the future in 1740 is the willingness of a segment of opinion to believe that the king was involved in the famine plot against his own subjects. In this extreme view the king was blamed not in the passive sense in which the leader must bear moral responsibility for what-

---

On crie publiquement notamment le petit peuple contre les intendans de Lille, Valenciennes et Artois, qu'ils accusent dans le public sans ménagement d'avoir fait sortir des grains sans nombre pour les depotes en Pays étrangers et les faire revenir, qu'ils le font en effet, et les vendent à demy-gatés à un prix excessif et qu'ils senrichissent de cette maniére aux depens même de la vie de ceux à la conservation desquels ils sont chargés de veiller, ce qui fait échaper le peuple en bien des plaintes amères et des injures, quand il est irrité, il est toujours bien mauvais de la langue, lorsqu'il ne peut l'être de fait il ne ménage personne.

Bultel to PG, 2 August 1740, Coll. JF 1123, fol. 27. Cf. suspicions emanating from Angoulême directed against the intendant Tourny. 10 May 1739, Coll. JF 1120, fols. 59–61.

[257] CG to Pallu, 5 October 1740, KK 1005F, AN.

[258] CG to Pallu, 14 October 1740, KK 1005F, AN; CG to des Gallois de la Tour, 2 November 1740, ibid.; CG to Jomarron, 1 November 1740, ibid.; CG to Vanolles, 6 November 1740, ibid.

ever calamities befall his nation, but in the active sense of having planned and implemented the dearth for venal motives. His corruptness was linked by some to his sexual debauchery and his lavish way of living, and it was suggested that he was unfit to rule. There were even reports of threats made against his life.[259]

There were lesser degrees of royal incrimination. There was the fiscal indictment, also applied to Fleury and Orry, that if the king was manipulating subsistence it was not for his personal aggrandizement but in order to replenish the coffers of the government treasury.[260] Even if Louis were not directly or materially guilty of conspiracy or manipulation, his conduct horrified observers. Barbier lamented "the indifference of the king for these catastrophes." "Yet the king is losing his reputation more and more," noted d'Argenson, "he sees his kingdom perish and instead of doing anything he lets things go as they are."[261]

There was yet another interpretation of the king's conduct, far more sympathetic to him, and it appears to have had considerable currency. In this scenario the king was either unaware of the true situation or lied to and duped by Fleury and Orry.[262] This view implies a portrait of Louis XV that is not very flattering: at best a monarch totally isolated from the everyday realities of the kingdom, dependent upon his ministers for all news and bereft of any independent means of verification;[263] at worst, inordinately naive and malleable, incompetent, perhaps idiotic. In either case he bore little resemblance to the *héros nourriciers* with whom kingship had been traditionally associated.

The only institution that competed with the king for claim to the title of father of the people, the Paris Parlement, also appeared prominently in the famine plot persuasion for the first time in 1740.[264] As with the monarch, there were several different perceptions. For one fraction of opinion, the *parlementaires* were no less guilty than the Orry brothers. "It was not surprising," one group of Parisians was reported to have argued, "that the controller-general dared to undertake to reduce the kingdom to a general

---

[259] Gazetins de police, 16, 19, 25 September 1740, MS. Bast. 10167, fols. 132-133, 136-137, 145.

[260] 8 October 1740, ibid., fol. 189, and 29, 30 September 1741, ibid., 10168, fol. 333.

[261] *Journal de Barbier* (ed. 1858), 3: 219 (September 1740); d'Argenson, *Journal*, ed. by d'Argenson, 2: 182 (10 July 1740); d'Argenson, *Journal*, ed. by Rathery, 3: 224 (14 November 1740).

[262] Gazetins de police, 26 September, 18, 21, 22 October, 14 December 1740, MS. Bast. 10167, fols. 145, 161, 166, 195; d'Argenson, *Journal*, ed. by Rathery, 3: 172 (September 1740); *Journal de Barbier* (ed. 1858), 3: 246-247 (December 1740); Narbonne, *Journal*, p. 485. The king was said to have had a dream about four cats. One of his bodyguards interpreted it for him as follows: the blind cat was Louis XV, the suspicious-looking cat Fleury, the fat cat Orry, and the starveling cat the people. Gazetins, 15 April 1741, MS. Bast. 10168, fol. 122.

[263] Narbonne recounted that Orry told the king that the price of bread was 3 sous when in fact it was 4 1/2 sous, "and not one of the seigneurs present had the courage to tell the truth to the king." *Journal*, p. 485. Barbier relates a strikingly similar episode but in his version one courtier boldly announced that bread was at 5 sous. *Journal de Barbier* (ed. 1858), pp. 246-247 (December 1740).

[264] It would be tempting to argue that the Parlement, like the king in 1725, was still something of a minor, having only recently returned from its long crossing of the desert. But even during its eclipse, it continued to exercise the "grande police" over the capital.

dearth" because he could count on the support of the "grands seigneurs" and the leading magistrates of the parlement "who profitted from this opportunity to enrich themselves." To cover the plot the parlement issued decrees announcing that the dearth was "natural" and "inevitable" whereas in fact it was of their own making. Further proof of the guilt of the parlementary leaders, the first president and the procurator general, was found in their failure to open an independent investigation of the causes of the dearth as the court had done in the past. Thus they "have abandoned the cause of the people, though they are their natural fathers."[265] At antipodes was another theory that the parlement was awaiting the appropriate moment to recall the king to his duty by showing him, in a stinging remonstrance, that his predecessors "had never allowed the lives of their subjects to be given a price as a consequence of grain speculation."[266]

---

[265] Gazetins de police, 19, 25, 29 September 1740 and 4 January, 3 October 1741, MS. Bast. 10167, fols. 137, 142, 147 and 10168, fols. 34, 338. The arrêts referred to were those of September 1740 limiting bakers to two sorts of bread, prohibiting brewers from making beer for a year, and forbidding tanners or starchmakers to utilize grain that could be used in baking. 5 February 1741, H 1859, fols. 204–207, AN; Conseil Secret, 22 September 1740, X^{1a} 8468, AN; Coll. JF 1120, fols. 248–251. The same legislation had been passed in 1725. Conseil Secret, 21 August 1725, X^{1a} 8446.

[266] Gazetins de police, 18, 19, 28 October 1740, MS. Bast. 10167, fols. 161, 185. The parlement evoked the "calamities" of the dearth in passing in its remonstrances against the dixième. 6 September 1741, J. Flammermont and M. Tourneux, eds., Remontrances du Parlement de Paris au dix-huitième siècle (Paris, 1888–1898), 1: 377–383. The parlement was also engaged at this time in an unseemly brawl with the Chambre des comptes over the management of funds destined "for the subsistence of the poor." 8 January 1741, Gazetins, MS. 620, BHVP; Maurepas to LG, 12 January 1741, 3 AZ 10^2 pièce 5, Arch. Seine-Paris.

III. The Dearths of 1747 and 1751-1752

Following the crisis of 1738–1741, there ensued almost a quarter century of relative ease in subsistence. To be sure, there were occasional regional and local difficulties. From our perspective, the most interesting case occurred during the dearth that struck the Bordeaux area in 1747. The Controller-General Machault, a strong-willed interventionist like his predecessor Orry, decided to take direct charge of relief efforts. First he annulled the measures taken by the intendant Tourny, a highly regarded administrator. Second, he dispatched his close friend Etienne-Michel Bouret to organize provisioning operations on the spot.[267] From the vantage point of public opinion, Machault could not have made a more unfortunate choice of emissaries, for Bouret was a farmer-general whose notorious prodigality, influence-dealing, and financial speculations rendered him highly suspect.[268] In short order, as prices remained elevated and emergency grain arrived slowly, Bouret found himself accused by leading public figures as well as by simple consumers of trying to establish "an odious monopoly." The Bordeaux Parlement bitterly criticized Bouret's "company" and launched a formal inquiry into reports of price manipulation, hoarding, malversation, and sales of rotten grain capable of "poisoning the people." The royal council's attempt to quash the investigation merely heightened the parlement's conviction that the government had something sordid to hide.[269]

Machault was still controller-general during another eruption of famine plot apprehensions in Paris in 1751–1753. In response to a short crop in 1751, the government arranged for the importation of foreign grain and set up storage depots in more than a dozen places in the Paris supply zone. It is possible that there was already a residue of government grain on hand from previous victualing campaigns.[270] Before the onset of winter, field agents disposed of king's grain with the aim, in the words of one, "of putting myself in a position to regulate the price on the markets." That policy implied blitzkrieg tactics of the sort that the central government had usually deplored, and it is no surprise that this agent was rebuked for

---

[267] Marion, "Une Famine en Guyenne," pp. 246–248 and *passim*.

[268] On Bouret, see P. Clément, *M. de Silhouette, Bouret, les derniers fermiers-généraux; études sur les financiers du 18e siècle* (Paris, 1872) and Y. Durand, *Les Fermiers-Généraux au 18e siècle* (Paris, 1971).

[269] Parlement of Bordeaux, representations to king, Fall 1748, C 1439, AD Gironde.

[270] Foucaud to PG, 18 June 1752, Coll. JF 1113, fol. 189; anon., "Mémoire," 1760, F¹¹ 1194, AN; Marion, *Machault d'Arnouville. Etude sur l'histoire du contrôleur général des finances de 1749 à 1754* (Paris, 1891), pp. 431–432; anon., "Mémoire," 1761, MS. fr. 11347, fols. 217–218, BN; *Mémoires de Luynes*, 11: 467 (March 1752); Béguillet, *Traité des subsistances*, p. 5.

selling the king's grain too cheaply.[271] Circumspection must have prevailed, for prices remained high—between 50 and 100 percent above their pre-scarcity levels—even after the harvest of 1752, which was generally es-teemed to be good, especially for wheat, in both quality and quantity.[272]

Once again it was this paradox of high prices amid (apparent) abundance that called forth the plot persuasion. "It is supposed," wrote Barbier, "that the high price of bread . . . results from some maneuver, since there is no *real* dearth."[273] As in previous instances, it was charged that grain hoards were being formed throughout the realm and that *laboureurs* were kept from the market in order to permit the official commissioners to sell king's grain of bad quality at extortionate prices. The authorities tried to discount these charges on the grounds that they emanated from "the malevolence of the ill-intentioned"—another kind of plot—but they conceded that these rumors were widely believed.[274] "The word spreads everywhere that the king is involved in the grain trade," noted d'Argenson," and since the price keeps mounting every day despite the abundance of the harvest, that pro-duces a dangerous effect."[275] D'Argenson solemnly warned that such ma-nipulations fatally lead to "revolts" in which those responsible "get torn to shreds."[276] Revolts had already jolted Rouen and towns in Auvergne, Provence, and Dauphiné, and posters in the capital threatened to "ravage" the city and burn all the bakeshops if the government did not immediately reduce the bread price.[277]

This installment of the famine plot history is slighter than earlier ones, in part because less evidence has survived, but it still contains most of the standard elements or recognizable proxies. According to d'Argenson, Ma-chault (who seems to have had no egregious personal flaw) was "pushed" to become a "grain merchant" by the "gens de finance" and "the friends of the marquise de Pompadour," in particular by his intimate Bouret, who devised a scheme that promised to benefit the state and the king as well as the conspirators. To "disguise the monopoly in the garb of public good," continued d'Argenson, the controller-general commissioned a victualing

---

[271] Missonnet to PG, 12 June 1752 and Gaudet to PG, 2 October 1752, Coll. JF 1112, fols. 92, 142. Compare Orry's pricing principle with Missonnet's idea: "One must not fear a loss when one sees that it could result in a diminution of the grain price." To PG, 17 July 1752, ibid., fol. 107.

[272] On the harvests, see Missonnet's and Foucaud's reports, Coll. JF 1113, fols. 22, 193–196. On the prices in Bray, Provins, Nogent-sur-Seine, and Montereau, see Coll. JF 1112 and in Gonesse, Beaumont, Pontoise, Meulan, Magny and Chaumont, see J. Dupâquier, *et al.*, *Mercuriales*, pp. 188–191.

[273] *Journal de Barbier* (ed. 1858), 5: 226, 313 (May and December 1752).

[274] Missonnet to PG, 18 September, 2 October 1752, Coll. JF 1113, fols. 135, 143.

[275] D'Argenson, *Journal*, ed. by d'Argenson, 4: 99–100 (27 August 1752). Cf. d'Argenson, *Journal*, ed. by Rathery, 7: 312 (3 October 1752): "The rumor is abroad in Paris that the king is profiteering in grain." D'Argenson suggested that the harvest of 1752 was one of the best in the last half-century. *Journal*, ed. by Rathery, 2: 446 (6 April 1753).

[276] D'Argenson, *Journal*, ed. by Rathery, 7: 286, 307–308 (27 August, 21 September 1752).

[277] On the Rouen riot, see *Mémoires de Luynes*, 11: 499–501 (26 April 1752). For the Paris posters, 20 March 1752, MS. Bast. 10139 and the multiple *plaintes* addressed to commissaire Machurin on 20, 21, 29 March 1752, Y 12596, AN.

company, run by Bouret's associates in the general farm and the banking milieu, to establish granaries throughout the kingdom to be used ostensibly to combat dearth. The company plundered the surplus areas of all their grain not for the purpose of meeting future needs but rather to prolong the current shortage. Given its institutional granary role, the company would presumably be in a position to bilk the nation whenever it so desired by instigating phony dearths.[278]

D'Argenson claimed that rumors implicating ministers, intendants and their clerks in grain manipulations were rampant everywhere.[279] In at least two places they threatened to have disturbing political consequences. The Parlement of Rouen protested against the provisioning practices undertaken in the king's name and suggested that they may have had something to do with the conditions that led to the violent riot of April 1752. It took quite seriously the stories of grain tossed in the Seine at night to boost prices and of clandestine stocks protected by the intendant. The ministry sternly warned the magistrates against spreading "false ideas" and quashed a decree by which the court hoped to control large-scale grain dealings in its jurisdiction.[280]

The Paris parlementaires followed in the muckraking tracks of their Norman colleagues. In December 1752 the abbé Vougny, a forty-seven-year-old counselor in the Grand' Chambre with a reputation as a reformer, wanted to denounce the grain perfidies in an open debate and to have the parlement send a committee to investigate the operation of the police and the grain trade in the major hinterland markets. He intimated that there were eighty "extraordinary grain storehouses" that had no legal charter. The ministry labored hard to silence Vougny, but if his impassioned appeal won insufficient support within the parlement it was because the magistrates were preoccupied with the bitter Jansenist controversy (which would lead shortly to their exile) and because the idea of such inflammatory action on the delicate subsistence issue frightened them.[281]

As in 1725 and 1740, there were certain elements of *vraisemblance* that help us to fathom the conspiratorial mentality. Even as Pompadour served as a shadowy surrogate for the far more indiscreet Madame de Prie and Bouret as an analogue of Fulvy and the Pâris brothers, so, too, the Indies Company (or the Monster-Bank) had its counterpart in the so-called "vic-

---

[278] D'Argenson, *Journal*, ed. by Rathery, 7: 277-278, 284-285, 307-308, 321, 326-327, 388-390 (13, 27 August, 21 September, 9, 19 October 1752 and 21, 22 January 1753); d'Argenson, *Journal*, ed. by d'Argenson, 4: 99-100 (27 August 1752).

[279] D'Argenson, *Journal*, ed. by Rathery, 7: 225 (7 May 1752).

[280] A. P. Floquet, *Histoire du Parlement de Normandie* (Rouen, 1840-1842), 6: 414-419; d'Argenson, *Journal*, ed. by Rathery, 7: 278 (13 August 1752); Marion, *Machault*, 432; G. Lemarchand, "Les Troubles de subsistances dans la généralité de Rouen," *Annales historiques de la Révolution française*, 35 (October-December 1963): 410.

[281] *Journal de Barbier* (ed. 1858), 5: 313-314 (December 1752). According to d'Argenson, "the people" hailed the court's "patriotic initiatives." But he also took note of a poster threatening to burn Paris if the parlement did not arrange to have bread prices lowered. *Journal*, ed. by Rathery, 7: 353-354 (12 December 1752). On Vougny, see also *Mémoires de Luynes*, 9: 480 (8 September 1749) and Bluche, *L'Origine des magistrats*, p. 411.

tualing company," which d'Argenson maintained was the same as the
military provisioning or *étapes* company. D'Argenson, Vougny, and other
contemporaries in fact muddled and misread two different realities, but in
a way that is not hard for us to understand. There was indeed an emergency
victualing enterprise mounted to import grain and it managed to stay out
of the limelight. It was run by Gabriel Bouffé, a shipping magnate, banker,
and international trader, and by Isaac Vernet, the inevitable Protestant
banker, who was also an associate of Dominique d'Héguerty, one of Isaac
Thellusson's partners in certain grain ventures in the late thirties. Between
1751 and 1753, this company spent at least 2,739,331 livres on grain operations, and probably much more.[282] Unlike Orry, Machault did not appear
to have become personally involved in the supervision of this campaign.
He delegated responsibility to Gaudet, a senior clerk in the *vingtième* department, who remained a central figure in the grain bureau for many
years. In addition to directing the foreign grain operation, Gaudet may also
have organized purchases in the interior. He had charge of the myriad
grain magazines set up as storage and distribution posts in the Paris supply
zone. While Gaudet remained utterly inconspicuous in his handling of
grain affairs, plot believers and cynics might have been gratified to know
that he was later charged by government auditors with serious irregularities
in his provisioning accounts.[283]

The other company—the *étapes*—also existed, albeit fleetingly, and while
some of its grain may have ended up in the public marketplaces, it had
nothing to do with the dearth-service in 1752. Struck with the extraordinary
vulnerability of the kingdom during subsistence crises and the enormous
cost of dealing with them more or less frenetically after they broke out,
Machault contemplated some sort of insurance in the form of an emergency
grain reserve. He signed an agreement at the end of 1750 with the entrepreneurs of the *étapes*—the military victualers—requiring them to establish
civilian granaries under the cover of their army storehouses. There they
were to hold at the constant disposition of the government thousands of
muids of grain ready for responding to crises on short notice. Within about
a year Machault annulled the contract when he learned that the company
was abusing its authority by engaging in speculative buying, farming out
its granary obligations to subcontractors, and disrupting the grain trade in
several areas. It is easy to see how contemporaries might have associated
the *étapes* enterprise with the dearth, especially since its initial operations
coincided with the bad harvest of 1751.[284] If the very existence of this
company was not enough to raise grave suspicions, let us take note of the

---

[282] F[11] 1191–1192, AN; Lüthy, *Banque* 2: 223–224. Leprévost de Beaumont denounced Vernet
and Bouffé as Machault's henchmen in his sweeping exposure of the famine plot. MS. Bast.
12353. On the magnitude of the purchases, see Dupont, *Analyse historique*, pp. 97–98.

[283] "Réponse du Sr Gaudet," January 1769, F[11] 1192, AN; *Almanach royal* (1761), p. 163; F[11]
1194, AN; Gaudet to (?), 16 January 1769, F[11] 223, AN; Missonnet to PG, 12 June 1752, Coll.
JF 1112, fol. 92.

[284] "Extrait historique de l'engagement contracté par les étapes en 1750," F[11] 647, AN; Dupont,
Analyse historique, pp. 94–98; Marion, *Machault*, pp. 430–432.

rumor that its titular head was an old hand in victualing affairs, Pompadour's father Poisson.[285]

Two other matters seemed to give credence to the plot accusations. First, it was widely known that the government needed money in the fall of 1752 even more desperately than usual.[286] Second, there was again considerable evidence that some of the king's grain was of very dubious quality. To the chagrin of the royal grain agents, the local hinterland police were the first to denounce the government grain as "rotten and defective." At Provins, they even threatened to arrest the merchant commissioned to sell this grain. Even when the price of king's grain was "very much below" *laboureurs'* wheat, the consumers were reluctant to buy it, so suspicious were they of its quality. "It is a mania or rather a blindness that I cannot comprehend," wrote one of the central government's representatives.[287]

---

[285] D'Argenson, *Journal*, ed. by Rathery, 7: 278 (18 August 1752). Cf. Barbier's kind remark about this "*original* who drank too much and was the first to joke about the high fortune of his daughter." *Journal de Barbier* (ed. 1858), 6: 37 (June 1757).

[286] Jobez, *Louis XV*, 4: 345-346.

[287] Missonnet to PG, 12 June, 14 August 1752, Coll. JF 1112, fols. 93, 120. Missonnet suggested that the police had a vested interest in discrediting grain that competed with grain owned by their families and friends. On forcing the public to eat rotten grain in 1752, see anon., "Mémoire," 1761, MS. fr. 11347, fols. 317-318, BN; Picque to PG, 15 May 1752, Coll. JF 1129, fols. 14-15; and d'Argenson, *Journal*, ed. by Rathery, 7: 277 (13 August 1752).

IV. The Crisis of 1765-1770

The famine plot persuasion erupted again in the mid-1760s and it became a quasi-permanent mental set for the next ten years, the most turbulent decade in the reign of Louis XV. The occasion was a grave and prolonged dearth that appeared to many contemporaries to have been planned and sustained by the government. The climate was ideally suited for the propagation of the famine plot persuasion as a result of two radical measures promulgated in 1763 and 1764 by which the royal government renounced the stewardship over subsistence that it had exercised, so it seemed, from time immemorial. Heretofore the monarchy had been unequivocally committed to a policy of fostering the provisioning of the grain markets, in large measure as a guarantee of social stability. In order to make sure that grain was supplied regularly, in suffcent amounts of adequate quality, and at a price accessible to the mass of buyers, the grain trade was subject to a host of controls and regulations. This "police" of provisioning was one of the major preoccupations of authorities at every level of public life. The "liberalization" laws of 1763-1764 freed the grain trade by dismantling the entire police apparatus in the name of the natural rights of proprietors and the political economy of growth. The royal government broke its unwritten covenant with consumers and proclaimed that henceforth subsistence was a matter for them to work out on their own.[288]

Liberalization led to a severe subsistence crisis that turned into a general crisis, at once socioeconomic, political, intellectual, moral. Liberalization, by its very nature, mimicked many of the effects of dearth. By openly encouraging speculation and higher prices, enabling new hands to enter the trade ("strangers"), permitting commercial associations ("companies"), promoting secret transactions, and forbidding the police to repress these practices that had till now been considered heinous anti-social crimes, the reform laws resulted in a breakdown in the supply system. As markets were abandoned and prices rose, "panic terror" set in among buyers, aggravating the disorganizing consequences of liberalization. Then came a series of mediocre-to-disastrous harvests that made matters far worse. Both in terms of causes and effects, it became impossible to disentangle liberalization from the shortage or, to put it in the language of the time, to distinguish the real dearth from the artificial one. The deepening subsistence crisis, bringing economic stagnation, unemployment, and misery in its wake, provoked a political crisis from below and from above. From below: consumer uprisings occurred throughout the kingdom and were

---

[288] For the reasons that motivated the government to take this daring and parlous step, see Kaplan, *Bread, Politics and Political Economy*, chap. 3.

frequently tolerated or even supported by the local police who, in this fashion, rioted against the liberal laws that tied their hands. From above: the coalition of the people and the police was reinforced by several parlements, a number of intendants, and a group of philosophes.[289]

If he could prevent disorder in Paris, Laverdy, the controller-general, believed that he was politically strong enough to force grain to be free in the rest of France. One of the ways he hoped to neutralize the capital was by maintaining a secret fund of king's grain that could be called upon in emergencies without undermining the freedom of the grain trade that reigned elsewhere. This granary was operated by a newly established company headed by an entrepreneurial ex-baker named Malisset and backed by three affluent royal officials with experience in financial affairs and in international commerce. The contract signed by Laverdy carefully safeguarded royal interests; the company had onerous responsibilities and no prospect of windfall profits. But, within certain limits, the company was free to speculate in grain and flour. It is likely that Malisset flourished the royal name in order to facilitate the company's private business. This may account in part for the astonishing proliferation of rumors concerning an alleged "royal grain monopoly" in the late sixties. Even without Malisset's indiscretions, however, it is doubtful that the company's operations could have been conducted clandestinely, for as the crisis worsened, Laverdy was obliged to call increasingly upon the company for assistance.[290] While the Malisset company was extremly active, it simply could not have been everywhere that it was allegedly espied and denounced. Scores of other grain companies, managed by influential men such as the financier Billard and the farmer-general Jausse, which had nothing to do with the king's granary, were assimilated in observers' minds to the Malisset enterprise.[291] It is easy to see how the royal company was puffed into the shape of a grasping, ubiquitous monster sucking the nation's lifeblood. Ironically, instead of serving as a safety-valve, the royal company helped to discredit the government and to undermine liberalization.

---

[289] On the general crisis and its ramifications, see ibid., chapters 5-6.

[290] On the contract, see ibid., 1: 356 ff. Malisset was by no means the first government-sponsored victualer who exasperated or embarrassed officials with his indiscretion, though he may have been the most significant single case. See the complaints of the Paris municipality against the conduct of Sieur Tellès, banker and international grain trader, associate of the Pâris brothers, who was commissioned to supply grain in 1729: "Il [Tellès] a dit que ces grains venoient par ordre du Roy. Vous scavés l'attention que nous avons eüe d'empecher que les grains que nous avons fait venir ne paroissent être pour le compte du Roy, et combien de pareils bruits sont capables de faire tort aux bonnes intentions que l'on a. Il faut que ceux qui amenent ces grains ne paroissent sur les ports que comme des marchands." Lambert to Hérault, 19 March 1729, MS. Bast. 10005.

[291] On the Jausse company, in which a secrétaire du roi and an "intéressé dans les affaires du roi" also participated, see 30 July 1764, D3B⁶ 65, Arch. Seine-Paris. On the Billard company, see 18 December 1768, Coll. JF 1138, fols. 92–93; Conseil Secret, 29 December 1769, X¹ᵃ 8551, AN; 16 December 1769, Y 11441, AN. Royal mistresses and financiers had a mutual faible and need for each other. Billard was a protégé of Madame du Barry who helped him to escape harsh punishment in a fraudulent bankruptcy case. Hardy's Journal, 3, 12 February 1772, MS. fr. 6681, pp. 15, 19, BN.

In the fall of 1768, when bread had risen to twice its normal price, seditious posters began to appear on the walls. One, judged by a commissaire to be the work of "Gens de Peu de Chose," admonished Louis XV to "get rid of Mssrs. Choiseul and Laverdy, who with a troop of thieves cause grain to be taken outside the Kingdom" or else thirty thousand men would do the job for him at an unexpected moment.[292] Another poster expressed profound disenchantment with the king, reproaching him for abdicating the traditional paternalistic kingship and darkly hinting that he had a venal interest in prolonging the suffering of his subjects:

Under Henri IV we suffered a dearth of bread occasioned by the wars but during this time we had a king; under Louis XIV we similarly experienced several other dearths of bread, produced sometimes by the wars, sometimes by a real shortage caused by the inclemency of the seasons, but we still had a king; in the present time the dearth of bread can be attributed neither to wars nor to a real shortage of grain; but we don't have a king, for the king is a grain merchant.

The poster concluded by recalling the assassination attempt that Damiens made upon the king in 1757, intimating that such a fate would not be unworthy of the apostate-monarch and that men capable of such a murder were prepared to act.[293]

Wall posters worried the government but Laverdy would not have regarded the famine plot insinuations as truly dangerous had they merely been effusions of popular fear and suspicion. But, as he wrote to the intendants with the aim of mobilizing them to assist him in exposing the famine plot persuasion as an error, "it has spread among the People and even among the most enlightened persons that different companies, several of which even protected by the government, had a part in this price rise through large, indiscreetly-made purchases."[294]

Among these enlightened persons who entertained suspicions were a number of intendants, the highest royal officials in the provinces. Their most vocal spokesman was Cypierre, intendant of the Orléanais, a generality to the south of Paris in a fertile grain-producing area. He believed that "a privileged Company" abusively operating behind the shield of royal authority, was responsible for the dearth. "The price rise, Monsieur," he

---

[292] Roland to PG, 21 Sept. 1769, Coll. 1139, fol. 54.

[293] Roland to PG, 31 October 1768, Coll. 1139, fol. 56; *Hardy's Journal*, 31 October 1768, MS. fr. 6680, p. 183, BN. Damiens, the king's assailant in 1757, insisted repeatedly during his interrogations that he had been moved to act by "the misery of the people." Bread at that moment in the capital was 50 percent above its "normal" price. Mme *** to Mr de Mopinot, 6, 12 June 1757, in *Revue de Paris*, 12th year, 3 (15 June 1905): 771–772. Cf. Michelet, *Histoire de France*, 15: 322–354. In the same chapter in which he discussed the Damiens attack, Michelet evoked the "legends" of the famine plot and the *parc aux cerfs* (where the king's enormous grain profits enabled him to keep 1,800 girls, mostly adolescent virgins).

[294] CG to Cypierre, 26 September 1768, cited by C. Bloch, "Le Commerce des grains dans la généralité d'Orléans," *Etudes sur l'histoire économique de la France (1760–1789)* (Paris, 1900): 46–47. Cf.: ". . . those who make the most rumor are the persons above the people whose fear causes them to speak indiscreetly in front of their valets." Miromesnil to CG, 21 March 1768, in P. LeVerdier, *Correspondance politique et administrative de Miromesnil, premier président du Parlement de Normandie* (Paris, 1899–1903), 5: 129.

informed the controller-general, "has other causes than the ordinary depletion of the old grain. I repeat, it is the result of maneuvers of this Company which has made itself master of the supply." What scandalized and frustrated this indendant was that the liberal laws prohibited him from taking any action. "These purchases," Cypierre complained, "were made by agents whom we could not question without appearing to infringe upon the liberty of the trade."[295] Local officials in the Paris supply zone had similar views. Barat, fiscal procurator at St.-Denis, wrote that it was generally believed that the dearth was the work of "certain companies that undertake exportation." Trennin, a police official at Versailles, and Desromont, royal procurator at Montlhéry, echoed the idea that "the companies" engineered the crisis.[296]

Meanwhile the magistrates of the Parlement of Rouen picked up the scent of the Company and pursued it tenaciously. In April 1768 a member of a committee named by the parlement to investigate the causes of the dearth claimed to have discovered that "there was in Paris a company which, under the pretext of provisioning the capital, has become master of this commerce in the whole realm." The goal of the company was "to starve out" whole provinces by buying all the grain in the markets and granaries and shipping it abroad to store (even as their counterparts in earlier times had cached their grain in the isles of Guernsey and Jersey), and then reimporting the same grain under a new name for a bountiful profit after prices had skyrocketed.[297] In October the magistrates sent a letter to Louis XV in which they virtually accused him of complicity in a "criminal" grain monopoly operating "in the shadow of a law [ostensibly] devised to prevent it." Enormous amounts of grain, noted the parlement, have been purchased "for the same account" in many markets. No "private enterprise" could handle such "immense" transactions: "There is only one Company whose members have sufficient influence to undertake such a thing. . . . Here we have recognized the imprint of power and the mark of authority."[298]

In November, at the same time that the Paris Parlement opened an inquiry of its own by subpoenaing Malisset (an interrogation that proved fruitless) and that several other sovereign courts began to address embarrassing questions to the government, the police arrested one Leprévost de Beaumont, who occupied the modest post of secretary to the general agent of the clergy. He had discovered a file of papers concerning the Malisset company and after connecting them with the widespread rumors of subsistence manipulation, he became convinced that he had found the trace

[295] Cypierre to de Montigny, 1, 7, 11 September 1768, in C. Bloch, *Le Commerce des grains dans la généralité d'Orléans d'après la correspondance inédite de l'intendant Cypierre* (Orléans, 1898), pp. 50, 63, 73–75; Cypierre to CG, 10 September 1768, ibid., p. 70; Cypierre to LG, 27 September 1768, ibid., p. 97.

[296] Barat to PG, 1 October 1766, Coll. JF 1134, fol. 93; Trennin to PG, 26 October 1768, Coll. JF 1142, fols. 162, 164.

[297] Miromesnil to CG, 30 April 1768, *Correspondance Miromesnil*, 5: 163–169 (two letters).

[298] Letter of 29 October 1768, Conseil Secret, 1767–1768, AD Seine-Maritime.

of "an infernal covenant of a monstrous league" whose goal was "to establish famine methodically in order to reap prodigious profits." The police arrested him after intercepting a fiery denunciation of the famine plot that Leprévost had mailed to the Rouen Parlement.

Leprévost portrayed Laverdy as the coordinator of a vast conspiracy that included officials and magistrates from the most august public bodies, assisted by a pack of other "pirates," "vultures," and "privileged vampires." Though he was not absolutely certain of the king's collusion, like the Rouen parlementaires, he suggested that the operation was too vast for the king to remain uninvolved and on several occasions he referred bitterly to "our monarch, merchant of grain." Using liberalization as a device to suppress controls without arousing suspicion and the permission to export as a pretext to hide huge quantities of grain abroad, the plotters stripped the kingdom bare of subsistence.[299]

Nor was the Laverdy plot the first of its kind. Leprévost traced the conspiracy back at least as far as Orry, and he blamed all the near-famines of the eighteenth century on the plotters. He did not appear to have known that similar cabals had been denounced periodically through the course of the century. His unawareness that suspicions like his had been articulated in previous times underlines how patterned the plot response was. Though there are many obvious similarities between the plot conceptions of the sixties and those of earlier times, from our perspective the indictment of the sixties seems to be informed by a sharper political consciousness and alienation. It focused much more on policies and institutions than upon individuals (such as depraved ministers, ravenous mistresses, corrupt hangers-on, and sly and avid court bankers). It fixed, in the words of the Rouen Parlement, on "the mark of authority" that was everywhere. More fully than the earlier accusations, those of the sixties developed the idea that the government had carefully prepared the conditions that generated the crisis and then exploited it shamelessly.[300]

Promised his release if he would agree to repudiate his charges, Leprévost chose instead, in the name of "my patriotic duty," to languish in the dungeons of the Bastille and other state prisons. The police considered him to be a madman, albeit a dangerous one, a demented subversive too articulate and too evangelical to be allowed to roam free. But to the revolutionaries who liberated him in 1789 after 21 years of captivity, it required no madness to envision the famine plot. Leprévost the martyr was living proof of the treachery and the inhumanity of the old regime. His revelations seemed particularly relevant at a time when the people lacked bread and on the morrow of the massacre of Foulon and Bertier de Sauvigny (once a patron of Malisset) by vengeful Parisians who accused them of conspiring to starve

---

[299] MS. Bast. 12353 and Leprévost de Beaumont, *Dénonciation d'un pacte de famine générale au roi Louis XV* (Paris, n.d.); *Dénonciation et pétition du sieur Le Prévôt de Beaumont* (Paris, 1791); *Dénonciation, pétition et rogation du sieur le Prévôt de Beaumont* (Paris, 1791).

[300] Kaplan, *Bread, Politics and Political Economy*, 1: 394–400.

the people.[301] No one was surprised to learn in 1789 that the counter-revolutionary famine conspiracy had its roots in the pre-revolutionary past.

Leprévost's story came full circle in 1794 during the high terror when he settled both a personal and a historical score. A gnarled old man was on trial before the Revolutionary Tribunal as a participant in "a plot" contrived by "the ferocious enemies of the Republic" to "effect a counter-revolution by starving the citizenry." His name: Laverdy, Leprévost's old nemesis, who had left public service just at the time of Leprévost's arrest and enjoyed a quarter-century of peaceful country retirement until the Revolution resurrected him. The evidence: a pit adjacent to his château in the Seine-et-Oise was found to contain enough buried grain to make 175,000 pounds of bread. The president of the court shifted attention from the present to the past: "Aren't you one of the authors of the famine plot of 1768?" Ill at ease, Laverdy tried to explain that the Malisset Company had been nothing more than an emergency granary that functioned in the public interest and with which he had had little to do. An incensed juror then sprang from the box to proclaim that he had personally witnessed employees of the company in 1768 throwing sacks of grain and flour into the river in order "to maintain a high price." At this point, a citizen entered the court and urgently demanded the right to testify. It was Leprévost, who proceeded to recount the horrors of the famine plot to a fascinated jury. The tribunal then adjourned, and after a short deliberation the president read the verdict: "That it is clear that there has existed a plot aiming to deliver the Republic to the horrors of famine by throwing into swamps or pools of water the grain necessary for the existence of the people in order to realize by this means counter-revolution and civil war. . . ." Laverdy was guillotined several hours later and Leprévost applied to the government for a portion of his famine-stained wealth as reparations for his twenty-one years of imprisonment.[302]

---

[301] Leprévost explicitly connected the famine plot of Bertier and Foulon with the earlier conspiracy of Laverdy. *Dénonciation et pétition du sieur Le Prévôt de Beaumont*, p. iii.

[302] *Bulletin du tribunal criminel et révolutionnaire*, 3 frimaire an II (nos. 99–100). Leprévost remained something of a cult figure well into the nineteenth century. He was the hero of several mawkish novels and plays that depicted him as a young patrician with populist ideas, defender of the miserable people against a cabal of corrupt plutocrats and officials. See, for example, Elie Berthet, *Le Pacte de famine* (Paris, 1857), and Berthet and P. Foucher, *Le Pacte de famine* (Paris, 1857).

V. The Crisis of 1771-1775

Though the royal government repudiated liberalization and returned to grain controls in 1770-1771, the famine plot suspicions persisted. Politically, the new controller-general, Terray, did not reap profit from this police restoration by demonstrating to the public how completely he had broken with the policies that many Frenchmen felt were responsible for the disasters of recent years. He allowed doubts to linger concerning his intentions, doubts that crystallized around his use of the king's grain.

As a result of the difficulties of transition from the chaotic liberal regime to a regulatory system and continued harvest failures, Terray felt obliged to intervene massively on the supply side. But there was to be no company, with all the implications of monopoly, privilege, and abuse, no contract, and no incoherence or contradiction in government policy. Unlike Laverdy, Terray had no doubts about the wisdom of engaging in public victualing whenever and wherever necessary. Like Orry, he supervised all provisioning operations vigilantly, working through a kind of public corporation called a *régie*. It inherited the physical facilities and the commercial network of the defunct Malisset Company. To manage the régie, Terray chose Daniel Doumerc, an experienced international grain trader, and Sorin de Bonne, a financier, military supplier, tax farmer, and sometime associate of the Pâris brothers. The régie functioned on a grander scale than had the Malisset enterprise, buying grain throughout France and the world over.[303]

Despite these changes, the king's grain operations remained shrouded in secrecy and the public perceived no discontinuity between the dealings of Malisset and those of Doumerc and Sorin. Local officials still talked about "the company" in the early seventies as if it were the same organization, motivated by the same spirit, as in the sixties.[304] There were the same anxieties about the bad quality royal grain and flour. Officials at Beauvais banned the use of régie grain because they claimed it imperiled public health; authorities in Champagne accused the régie of adulterating flour with chalk to enhance its allure to the eye.[305] The buying operations by the régie within the kingdom caused resentment, misunderstanding, and disorder in many areas. In a frank assessment of the problems encountered, the grain department, a branch of the controller-general's office, conceded:

---

[303] Kaplan, *Bread, Politics and Political Economy*, chaps. 12 and 13.

[304] Coll. JF 1158, fols. 81–96; letter of arbitre to juges-consuls, 29 March 1773, D6B⁶ carton 6, Arch. Seine-Paris.

[305] Coll. JF 1158, fols. 81–96; intendant of Champagne to Sorin and Doumerc, 31 December 1770, and Sorin and Doumerc to intendant, 12 January 1771, C 416, AD Marne.

the people became alarmed [and] even the courts and administrators complained and failed to cooperate; the precautions taken by the government were seen merely as an exclusive privilege accorded to individuals; justice was not done to the views which inspired the officials in charge; monopoly! was cried out, [though] unjust and without foundation, these cries produced fermentation which once born is very difficult to check.[306]

As in the sixties, famine plot rumors circulated throughout the realm. "It is true, Monsieur," one subdelegate declared to the intendant of Alençon "that the people attributed the dearth to the ridiculous idea that there existed a company exclusively charged with the provisioning trade of the entire kingdom."[307] The intendant of Brittany reported the existence of a "rumor" that "wins credence easily" concerning the operation of "a company which has the exclusive privilege to engage in grain commerce in the interior of the kingdom and which organizes surreptitious exporting."[308] In the spring of 1773 Hardy, the Parisian bookseller, noted in his diary "that the sieur abbé Terray, Controller-general of finances, suspected perhaps rightly of favoring the Monopoly and the Export of grain which occasioned the dearth and high prices in different provinces, could very well be cashiered. . . ."[309] The prediction was about a year premature.

What alarmed Terray in 1773 even as it had preoccupied Laverdy in 1767-1768 was that "the Bourgeoisie of the cities and even distinguished persons" as well as "the people" were "imbued with the false idea that there exists a company exclusively appointed to undertake the provisioning of the kingdom and the grain trade."[310] Events at Bordeaux provided the controller-general with the most striking example of this phenomenon. The Parlement of Bordeaux, like the Rouen court several years earlier, repeatedly denounced the existence of "a pretended Company in Paris which had the exclusive privilege for the grain supply of the kingdom."[311] In the local context, most of the charges pointed to the distinguished international banker and philanthropist, Bethmann. Of German origin and Protestant, Bethmann, like Samuel Bernard and Thelluson, was frequently called upon by the government to utilize his ability to marshal capital and his international connections in the public interest. There is little doubt that he participated in the régie grain operations as a gesture of good will rather than in the hope of speculative profits. Yet he found himself widely accused of belonging to "the company of Monopolists" that masterminded the dearth that afflicted the Bordelais and other provinces. His life and property menaced, he was obliged to hire twenty armed guards.

The famine plot accusations cost Bethmann the impeccable reputation that had taken forty years to make. "I must cleanse myself in the eyes of

---

[306] "Mémoire," 1773, C 1441, AD Gironde.

[307] Subdelegate at Argentau to intendant of Alençon, 13 October 1773, C 89, AD Orne.

[308] Intendant of Brittany to subdelegate at Nantes, 15 September 1773, C 774 and intendant of Brittany to CG, May 1774, C 1653, AD Ille-et-Vilaine.

[309] Hardy's Journal, 19 May 1773, MS. fr. 6681, p. 192, BN.

[310] CG to intendant of Picardy, 28 September 1773, C 86, AD Somme.

[311] CG to first president, Parlement of Bordeaux, 19 July 1772 and 5 November 1773, C 1441 and C 1442, AD Gironde.

all Europe of the crimes of which I am accused," he wrote to Terray, "and in order for me to do so you must lead the way." He demanded some sort of public declaration from the controller-general clearing his name and explaining the grain operation. Bethmann hinted cleverly and quite rightly that his own rehabilitation had important political implications. "It is in the state's interest to accord me what I desire, for this affair," Bethmann wrote, "to tell the truth, is really an affair of state." Beyond Bethmann, the famine plot rumors directly implicated the government. Sooner or later the ministry would have to face up to these "humiliating suspicions." By using his case as a vehicle, Bethmann reasoned, the government could offer a full explanation which would restore its credit in the public mind.[312]

Terray rejected Bethmann's lesson in public relations. Not only was the idea of appealing to public opinion repugnant to him, but he feared in any case that he would not be believed. His conception of paternalism precluded a dialogue between father and children. Terray remained impotent vis-à-vis the onslaught of the famine plot persuasion which, he acknowledged, made the government "more and more odious every day." All he could do was to philosophize on the tragic irony of the collective mentality. No matter what we do for the people, Terray observed, "they always believe that we wish to do them harm or that we neglect them." Terray resisted the temptation to abandon his subsistence policy in order to avoid casting further discredit on the government. His posture was courageous, even as his refusal to face the problem of public opinion squarely was obtuse. "It would be an inexcusable weakness," Terray wrote, "if the fear of evil gossip stopped the administration from acting for the public good as it can and as it must act."[313]

Terray was finally dismissed, to a considerable extent as a consequence of the famine plot charges, in 1774 immediately after the death of Louis XV. Like his controller-general, the king had suffered enormous discredit as a result of the famine plot charges. "Never was a prince less regretted than poor Louis XV," commented Moreau, a royalist lawyer-historian.[314] It is revealing of the power of collective memory that the same abusive epitaph that had once been chanted for the duc de Bourbon was now applied to Louis XV with a few minor modifications:

> Ci-gît le bien-aimé Bourbon
> Monarque d'assez bonne mine
> Et qui paye sur le charbon
> Ce qu'il gagne sur la farine[315]

If there were any lingering doubts about the authenticity of the plot

---

[312] Bethmann to CG, 25 May 1773, C 1441, AD Gironde.

[313] CG to Bethmann, 5 June 1773, ibid.; CG circular to intendants, 28 September 1773, AD Marne.

[314] J.-N. Moreau, *Mes Souvenirs*, ed. by C. Hermelin (Paris, 1898–1901), 1: 379. Cf. Métra: "The King has irretrievably lost the affection of his people." *Correspondance secrète, politique, et littéraire* (London, 1787–1790), 1: 16 (7 July 1774).

[315] Cited by Vicomte de Bastard d'Estang, *Les Parlements de France; essai sur leurs usages, leur organisation, et leur autorité* (Paris, 1857), 2: 508–509.

accusations, they were dissipated by Terray's successor, Turgot, intendant and philosophe, friend of the physiocrats and partisan of liberalization. In a series of resounding public statements, Turgot condemned all forms of public intervention in provisioning affairs and vowed never to permit his administration to encroach upon the freedom of commerce. Directly and indirectly, he gave credence to the idea that the Terray régie had indeed speculated and maneuvered and cheated.

To purge the government of the stigma of the famine plot, he ordered that the régie be dismantled. He fired the official in charge of Terray's grain department and used *lettres de cachet* to seize all the papers of the régie. One of Turgot's assistants, Albert, launched a sort of inquisition against Sorin and Doumerc that aimed to prove they were guilty of virtually everything with which popular rumor charged them. In any case, for Turgot and Albert, they were a priori culpable, condemned, as it were, by doctrinal error as much as by actual management.

Turgot once again freed the grain trade, imitating the great reforms of 1763. In May 1775 there erupted a series of violent riots throughout the Paris region, known to historians as the Flour War. Turgot rejected the idea that these uprisings, like those of the sixties, could be the result of popular subsistence difficulties caused in large measure by the new liberalization. Who then was responsible for these riots if they were not spontaneous manifestations of popular distress? Just as generations of Frenchmen had blamed the dearths they suffered on plots, so Turgot blamed the Flour War on a plot—one that curiously turns out to be merely another variation on the familiar theme. The Flour War, he suggested, was organized by his enemies, the former agents of the provisioning companies who lost everything when he came to power and cleaned out the Augean stables. These monopolists, supported perhaps by certain elements of the police, manipulated the people into mutinying against the government. Since these riots were as phony as the dearths that the monopolists used to cause, Turgot felt no compunction about repressing them brutally. At the same time he arrested Doumerc and Sorin who were presumably among the leaders in the conspiracy against him. Turgot's version of the plot thesis was in many ways the most sinister of all. The earlier versions merely discredited kings and ministers whereas Turgot's dishonored the people.[316]

---

[316] Kaplan, *Bread, Politics and Political Economy*, 1: 405–406, 2: 606–673. On the famine plot of the seventies and eighties involving the Leleu brothers, the victualers contracted by Turgot to replace Doumerc and Sorin, see F[11] 265, AN, and J. J. Rutledge, *Mémoire pour la communauté des maîtres boulangers de la ville et faubourgs de Paris, presenté au roi, le 19 février 1789* (N.p., n.d.) and *Second mémoire pour les maîtres boulangers* (Paris, 1789).

VI. Conclusion

Each episode of the famine plot persuasion is different from the others in its particular physiognomy, but a number of elements, in varying doses, seem common to all of its manifestations. The primacy and the sanctity or inviolability of subsistence are emphasized. The consumer-people is a blameless and easy victim, which makes the plot an especially heinous anti-social crime. The dearth is artificial. Since nothing is accidental and everything is laden with meaning, the slightest evidence (for example, guilt by association) or verisimilitude is extremely convincing. Influential, highly-placed persons, some of whom are in some way morally blemished (by cupidity, debauchery, Protestantism), are involved in the conspiracy, as are monster-like organizations (monopolies, companies, banks). There is a profound feeling of betrayal vis-à-vis the government. But the government is placed in a double bind. On the one hand its failure to act in the name of traditional values is taken as proof of its complicity in the plot, and on the other, when the government does intervene, its motives are suspect. The famine plot persuasion is not the preserve of one social group or one type of personality to the exclusion of others. It is remarkably pervasive. Nor is it peculiar to the eighteenth century.[317]

Why did the famine plot persuasion take such a deep hold of the French consciousness (and unconsciousness) in the old regime and become a durable part of the collective memory and mentality? The precipitants of the famine plot persuasion are relatively easy to discern. They are specific short-run or "conjunctural" factors that provoke stress, anxiety, disorganization. But what are its preconditions? What structural factors seem to invite or even compel belief in the famine plot?

The first point to insist upon is the tyranny of cereal-dependence in the pre- or proto-industrial world. Cereal-dependence conditioned every phase

---

[317] See, for example, the charges centering on J. Roger, a prominent Parisian grain merchant in the 1690s. MS. fr. 21642 (factum), BN. Or the people of Dijon during the dearth of 1531 who denounced the *échevins* as "grain merchants" who fabricated the scarcity in collusion with speculators. H. Hauser, "Une Famine il y a 400 ans," *Travailleurs et marchands de l'ancienne France* (Paris, 1920), pp. 118, 126. Or the speech of the Duke of Fitz-James concerning the French dearth of 1817 in which he excoriated the monopoly of famine-makers and warned of rumors that "the King and the Princes were the persons who sent our corn to England." London *Times*, 19 January 1818. See also L. Gueneau, "La Disette de 1816–1817 dans une région productrice de blé. La Brie," *Revue d'histoire moderne*, 19 (January–February 1929): 36–37. Local level research would doubtless reveal innumerable hometown versions of the famine plot. Nor was it peculiar to France. See, for instance, the accusations that the Dutch minister was in league with the merchants of Amsterdam and Rotterdam to starve the Belgians in 1815–1816. H. Pirenne, *Histoire de Belgique* (Brussels, 1926), 6: 274. See also P. A. Brunt, "The Roman Mob," *Past and Present*, no. 35 (December 1966): 3, 25, 26. On the potential for the development of a famine plot persuasion in the Third World, see the hints of James C. Scott, *The Moral Economy of the Peasant: Rebellion and Subsistence in Southeast Asia* (New Haven, 1976), p. 116n.

of social life. Grain was the pilot sector of the economy; beyond its deter-minant role in agriculture, directly and indirectly grain shaped the devel-opment of commerce and industry, regulated employment, and provided a major source of revenue for the state, the church, the nobility, and large segments of the third estate. Subsistence needs gave cereal-dependence its most telling expression. The vast majority of the people in the old regime derived the bulk of their calories from cereals, in bread or some other form. Because most of the people were poor, the quest for subsistence preoccupied them relentlessly. No issue was more urgent, more pervasively felt, and more difficult to resolve than the matter of grain provisioning. The dread of shortage and hunger haunted this society. Cereal-dependence produced a chronic sense of insecurity that caused contemporaries to view their world in terms that may strike us as grotesquely or lugubriously overdrawn.

Though they feared recurrent dearth, Frenchmen believed that France was an extremely rich nation capable of producing an abundant supply of grain. Given the inordinate richness of French arable, *ceteris paribus*, dearths should not have erupted as often as they did. This belief in abundance nurtured a conspiratorial turn of mind. It disinclined Frenchmen to blame shortages on natural disasters. Rather, they believed a priori that dearths were more often than not *un*-natural in their origins, the result of evil-doing along the path of distribution. In virtually every subsistence crisis observers denounced the intolerable and incriminating paradox of the co-existence of high or rising prices and abundant albeit hidden supplies, unmistakable proof of perfidy.

The police authorities reinforced this tendency to exonerate nature and indict human vice. They were reluctant to accept a naturalistic explanation because acknowledging publicly that a dearth was due to natural calamity was tantamount to confessing that it was beyond control. The authorities believed that such an avowal of helplessness would exacerbate difficulties by reinforcing the disaster cues received by the public. In addition, the police and the public shared a traditional distrust of commerce. The trader remained the prototype of the liar who menaced the well-being and the bonds of solidarity of society. The grain trader was especially odious, for who but vicious men would speculate on the subsistence of their fellow citizens? The general feeling was that if the grain trade were not vigilantly policed it would degenerate into monopoly, a vague and sweeping indict-ment of any sort of maneuver that reduced supplies and raised prices.

Given the uncertainties of production, the primitive means of commu-nication and transportation, the severe limits of conservation technology, the uninviting constraints imposed by the police, and the stigma attached to it by the public, the grain trade remained a highly underdeveloped and speculative activity.[318] The grain trade was unstable, spasmodic, unpre-

---

[318] In the eighteenth century the grain trade was highly speculative in large part because it was so underdeveloped in terms of markets, communication, production, and conservation technology. But the grain trade can remain a highly speculative activity long after drastic modernization. I'm thinking of the grain trade in America today. One striking recent example is the suspension of business on the Chicago Board of Trade in March 1979—an episode replete with charges of plots, monopoly, and scandal in the wheat futures market.

dictable, especially when it attempted to move beyond the immediate lo-
cality to cover significant expanses of space and time. Markets were badly
organized and inner-directed. Obstacles cluttered the road everywhere.
Even without the traditional prejudice against commerce, it is easy to see
how its operation could arouse suspicions among people who lived under
the tyranny of grain.

Structurally weak, the trading system easily broke down. It was taxed
with the greatest responsibilities at precisely the moments when it was
least able to meet them. Neither the public nor the police was indulgent
in these moments. Traders who failed to supply were monopolists plotting
to profit from the shortage they promoted. New men who appeared on the
scene were viewed with deep suspicion as speculators or vultures. Vision
became clouded in the dearth syndrome. Everywhere grain seemed to be
trying to flee, to be escaping. Single wagons swelled into great convoys in
the overheated popular imagination and nighttime departures became sure
signs of crime.

Remember, too, that public authorities tended to confirm popular suspicions and to reinforce what were contemptuously called popular preju-
dices. During times of troubles, declared the *économiste* Dupont, the police
"becomes people themselves."[319] Police officials, especially on the local level,
tended to see things in the same way as consumers. Indeed, in some instances the people took their cue from the police. This moral and psychological solidarity between the police and the people helped to lend credibility to the famine plot idea.

Nor were all these dark perceptions mirages or tricks that the threatened
stomach played upon the unschooled mind. The police at the local level
frequently uncovered in the grain trade what they called plots against the
public good. Moreover, people acquired hometown experience with plots
that involved prominent local citizens, very often police officials themselves, who could not resist the speculative lure of the grain trade, especially
in periods of disorganization. Viewed upon the background of the hometown experience, which taught people to expect to find local authorities
involved in secret trafficking, it is easier to understand the willingness of
Frenchmen to believe that more highly placed officials, with far greater
appetites and powers, could launch massive, illicit speculations on grain.
The idea that government could have some sinister connections with the
provisioning trade had solid local roots.[320]

---

[319] Dupont to Prince Karl Ludwig, 1773, in C. Knies, ed., *Carl Friedrichs von Baden Brieflicher
Verkehr mit Mirabeau und Dupont* (Heidelberg, 1892), 2: 146. Cf. Joly de Fleury: "Everyone is
people when they lack bread." Speech of 5 July 1763, *Recueil des principales lois*, p. 48.

[320] Police commissaire Delamare warned his agents in 1709 to pay special attention to the
activities of local authorities who "quite commonly undertake a sort of grain commerce."
Among those he accused were the president of the élection of Rozoy, the fiscal procurator of
Coulommiers, and the president of the présidial at Melun. *Traité*, 2: 925 and BN, MS. fr. 21645,
fols. 88, 210, 258, 423. The *substitut* at Vitry reported in 1725 that "almost all the officials" in
his area were clandestinely trading in grain. Domballe to PG, 25 October 1725, BN, Coll. JF
1116, fol. 280. At Rozoy-en-Brie in 1726, according to the commander of the maréchaussée, all
the officers of justice including the lieutenant general were regrating. Marchais to Hérault, 21
June 1726, MS. Bast. 10273. In 1748 a grain merchant formally filed a complaint with the

The fear of maneuvers and plots was heightened by a deep-seated subsistence particularism, itself a reflection and extension of a pervasive particularism that characterized all aspects of social, economic, political, and
cultural life. The subsistence world was a closed world. It was intensely
xenophobic. Strangers, outsiders—grain traders who came from other communities—were viewed as enemies. Locally cultivated grain was considered
to belong to the local citizenry. There was no sense of interdependence
with other communities. It is easy to see how an effort to mobilize surplus
grain could be misinterpreted by a self-absorbed hometown population.

Yet it might also be possible to view the famine plot persuasion as a
mark of the *failure* of this particularism to work effectively as a barrier
against change (or integration). For resistance to the intrusion of the market
in local life had proven to be futile in most instances (even if particularism
succeeded in retarding the development of regional markets). More and
more people had been or were being moved into the market. They had
become or were becoming dependent on forces they could neither fathom
nor control. The closed world was put under increasing economic and
political pressure both to renounce the familiar arrangements that had
governed its internal life and to renegotiate its relations with the outside.
Local officials themselves had an ambivalent attitude toward the extension
of the market. Often they took measures that simultaneously encouraged
and stifled its vitality. From this point of view, the famine plot persuasion
in certain towns and villages could be construed as a reaction—involving
a certain amount of displacement and personalization of blame—to the
corrosive process of market penetration. People became frightened and
troubled not because the market failed to work well but because it seemed
to work too well. In this perspective, the crisis of dearth appears as the
bacchanalian celebration of the triumph of the market rather than the
mourning of its collapse. The famine plotters were the promoters of the
market who knew how to turn it against the general good and exploit it
to their selfish advantage. The growth of this form of capitalism seemed
to violate the paternalistic ethos of the state.[321] This was not the least of the
contradictions of absolutism. The state proved to be a highly unreliable
protector of traditional values.

This parochialism was in part a result of bureaucratic underdevelopment
and insufficient national administrative integration. These in turn were

---

Châtelet against the fiscal procurator of Rambouillet for illicit speculations. AN, Y 11235 (18
October 1748). In 1774 another dealer pressed charges against the royal procurator of Pont
Sainte-Maxence for masterminding "odious maneuvers" in the grain market. Archives Seine-
Paris, 23 June 1774, D4B⁶ 52-3196. A bloody riot triggered by high bread prices jolted Toulouse
in June 1778. According to one observer, these high prices were caused by "the corruption
of the Capitouls and other officials." *Hardy's Journal*, 24 June 1778, MS. fr. 6683, p. 9, BN. There
had been earlier complaints of grain "maneuvers" by the Toulouse city fathers. De Vandour
to St.-Priest, 21 April 1773, C. 2914, AD Hérault.

[321] The famine plot persuasion reflected hostility to several other kinds of capitalism. Court
capitalism, represented by the Bernards and the Pâris, is one such strain that I have discussed.
Another is the vigorous opposition to the agri-business elite that manifested itself in the second
half of the century. On this theme, see Kaplan, *Bread, Politics and Political Economy, passim.*

partly the products of extremely poor communication systems. Everyone, the local government and the governed, suffered from a lack of reliable information. Everyone depended on rumors and hearsay. This kind of undocumented and uninformed information had an extraordinary power of mobilization. Witness, for a spectacular example, the contagion of the Great Fear, the rural panic of 1789. Erroneous news reports about the failure of harvests or about the peregrinations of beggars or brigands or the conscription of young men wreaked havoc throughout the old regime. Given the underlying insecurity concerning subsistence, any rumor touching the question was bound to have a profoundly unsettling effect.

To a large extent radically inadequate communications can be seen as ecological faults or structural weaknesses. But in part they were the products of political decisions. The history of the old regime is a history of a total failure of public relations. The failure was especially acute in the subsistence domain, where anxieties were so intense, emotions so volatile, and misinformation so rife. The government never made a serious effort to demystify and explain its policy and its action in the provisioning domain.[322] It allowed suspicions to swell and proliferate; by its silences, it tacitly lent them credence. To some extent this reticence bespoke the fear—not wholly unfounded—that the government would not be believed even if it told the truth. Yet it was primarily the fruit of a contempt for the people. Government was not their affair, not only because they were not intelligent or educated enough to apprehend its workings, but above all because it would be dangerous for a monarchy to suggest that it was in any way accountable to the public.

Commonly held expectations about subsistence helped to shape the collective mentality. To guarantee their well-being, the women of Paris marched on Versailles in October 1789 in order to bring back to Paris the baker, the baker's wife and the baker's boy. The king was considered the baker of last resort. According to the unwritten compact between king and people, in return for their submission, the king promised to assure them

---

[322] Yet see the singular gesture made, doubtless not without the ministry's approbation, during the time of Machault: "Il est arrivé néanmoins quelquefois que par un trop haut prix du bled dans tous les marchés des Provinces voisines de Paris comme des plus eloignées, l'on a soupçonné des manoeuvres illégitimes, & que tous les sages Réglemens ont été sans force à cet égard; mais dans ces derniers tems le Ministre du Commerce & des Finances a sçu imaginer un moyen immanquable pour faire cesser l'abus. Nous l'avons vû acheter des bleds chez l'Etranger, les faire ensuite verser & vendre, à la perte du Roi, dans différens marchés du Royaume, en abondance suffisante pour qu'on pût se passer des détempteurs injustes du bled national: bientôt ceux-ci souffrant dans le retard de leur débit, & ne pouvant plus espérer dans une survente l'effet de leur coupable cupidité, ont été obligés de ramener leur bled au prix convenable, & l'on a vu se rétablir ainsi l'équité & le bon ordre à cet égard. L'on sçait que cette opération faite en dernier lieu par M. le Garde des Sceaux, Controlleur Général des Finances, a coûté au Roi près d'un million; *mais l'on ne sçauroit rendre ces faits trop publics, afin d'exciter dans le coeur des Peuples de justes sentimens de reconnoissance pour la générosité paternelle du Roi, & les soins du Ministre qui en est le digne dépositaire.*" My italics. Le Camus, "Mémoire sur le bled," *Journal économique* (November 1753): 144–145.

their subsistence. In the last analysis, when something went awry in provisioning, the people held the government responsible. As an English observer remarked in 1763:

For since the people are made to depend upon the magistrates for a supply of their wants, they have a right to complain when a deficiency happens; and they will do so, even though the magistrates are in no way the cause of it. They that would command in fair weather must take to the helm in foul. . . .[323]

It was utterly in vain that a high royal official tried to persuade the women of October 1789 that the dearth was the product of bad weather and that "the king was no more capable of making wheat grow than of making it rain."[324] No, it was the king's duty to prevent subsistence crises or to attenuate them rapidly if they occurred. If the king and the government failed to act or (it amounted to the same thing) if the subsistence threat persisted or worsened, that was proof enough of some kind of plot. In the hypothesis most favorable to the king, the monarch is portrayed as the unknowing victim of a band of Rasputins. In the harshest hypothesis, he consciously betrays his own people.

The baker-king's solemn duty was not only to guarantee the supply. Abundance was necessary but by itself not sufficient. It had to be accompanied by accessible prices. *Cherté* and abundance—the physiocratic platform/shibboleth—was of no allure to the mass of consumers. Nor was there any practical distinction for them between *cherté* and famine. Grain (or bread) had to be offered at a fair or just price.[325] Scores of episodes of relatively orderly *taxation populaire* throughout the century testified to the deepseated popular conviction that prices had to respect imperious social needs. Price-making was perceived as a moral and political matter, ultimately an affair of state.

These specific subsistence expectations may have been reinforced indirectly and unwittingly by the general pattern of state development. The state attempted to implant itself in virtually every sphere of social life. It usurped functions that previously had been exercised by local or special

---

[323] W. Mildmay, *The Police of France*, p. 98. Cf. the complaint of the Dauphiné Parlement that "one of the most disastrous effects of the [police] regulations was to have habituated the People to hold the Government responsible for *cherté* or dearth." "Avis du Parlement de Dauphiné . . . au Roi," 26 April 1769, *Ephémérides du Citoyen* (1769), 1: 156.

[324] Baron de Barante, ed., *Mémoires de F. E. G., comte de Saint-Prest* (Paris, 1929), 2: 14–15. Cf. Voltaire on the subsistence mentality: "On accusait le ministère plutôt que la secheresse ou la pluie." Article "Blé ou Bled," *Dictionnaire philosophique*, in *Oeuvres complètes* (ed. Garnier, 1878), 18: 10. This mentality persisted well into the nineteenth century (and beyond): "Il est hors de doute que si le peuple manque de pain, il accusera l'administration publique d'imprévoyance; la colère germera dans son coeur; il croira aux accapareurs et même à la connivence des hommes d'Etat. Il faudrait donc avoir perdu le sens pour ne pas reconnaître que le premier souci des gouvernants est de veiller à ce que, en échange de son travail, la classe populaire soit toujours assurée de la vie suffisante." A. Corbon, *Le Secret du peuple de Paris* (Paris, 1863), p. 205.

[325] On the just price tradition, see Kaplan, *Bread, Politics and Political Economy*, 1: 58–59, 202, 306 and 2: 546, 612.

institutions. In some sense or other it managed religion, culture, the economy, and local and regional government. To be sure, absolutist aspirations,
or theory, far outstripped durable achievement. But the theory itself may
have had a significant impact. The state conditioned Frenchmen to view
the government as omnipotent. They were supposed to look to the center
as the unique source of authority and initiative. It followed that it was the
business of the government to foresee and resolve problems, and that it
was at fault when something of real importance went wrong. By breathing
new life into the ideology of paternalism, absolutism placed constraints on
the state's freedom of action that it was never able to overcome.

There is no doubt that government victualing operations bear a great
deal of the responsibility for promoting the famine plot persuasion. It is
easy enough to say in retrospect that had they been handled more effectively they would not have been such enormous political millstones. Given
all the other constraints that we have discussed, chances are that these
operations would have been politically disastrous even if they had been
managed with greater skill, economy, and circumspection. Large-scale buying operations in the interior were bound to cause market disorders and
provoke quite legitimate fears. Portions of imported grain were sure to be
spoiled, and bread made with well-conserved foreign grain was still likely
to have an unfamiliar and thus disquieting taste. Public victualing was
emergency victualing. It took place in crisis conditions and it was certain
to exacerbate the crisis in some ways even as it mollified it in others.[326]

Ultimately the problem was less with the management of buying operations than with the way they were perceived. For political as well as
commercial reasons, the government wanted the operations to be as inconspicuous as possible.[327] Yet it was virtually impossible to be discreet
about subsistence in a period of collective stress. The clumsy effort to maintain secrecy and the government's lack of candor troubled and puzzled
observers. Moreover, the few faces that the public caught glimpses of in
these operations were faces of well-known bankers or financiers, frequently
of unsavory reputation. It was easy to imagine that the grain that passed
through their hands was tainted.

For whom was this grain destined, after all, Frenchmen asked themselves.
If the king's grain was meant to relieve the crisis, why did it not have a
more telling impact? Consumers wanted instant gratification.[328] They were
interested neither in the laws of supply and demand nor in the strategy

---

[326] Obviously many Frenchmen did not appreciate the complexity and difficulty of large-
scale public provisioning. Witness the wistful and simplistic scenario sketched out in a counter-
revolutionary pamphlet. In trying moments of the old regime, it claimed, the father-king
"écrivoit à tous les rois ses voisins, les prioit de lui laisser acheter . . . du bled pour ses enfans.
. . ." Anon., *Sous un roi nous avions du pain* (Paris, ca. 1791). The government of the old regime
harbored no such illusions. See Delamare, *Traité*, 2: 599–600.

[327] See Linguet's dictum that "l'influence de l'autorité pour être efficace, doit être impercep-
tible." *Annales politiques, civiles et littéraires du dix-huitième siècle*, 7 (November 1779): 233.

[328] Here is the popular "analysis" of the way things ought to be, according to a public
opinion report of 1740: "Il est facille de faire manger le pain à un prix raisonable . . . si c'est

of royal provisioning. If the government intervened on the supply side in good faith, it should have been able to improve conditions more quickly. Lingering dearths and protracted royal provisioning campaigns suggested that something was not right. Moreover, government victualing was perforce discriminatory. The king's grain could not supply all the markets in the kingdom. And, if the government could not obtain all the grain that it needed abroad, it was obliged to make purchases in the interior (or, as it usually turned out, to plunder France in order to provide for Paris). The communities that were denied aid or those that were fleeced were deeply embittered and frustrated and easy prey to scapegoating, conspiratorial explanations.

Suspicions of victualing operations were enhanced by the distribution of surrogates such as the lesser cereals and rice. Numerous consumers clung tenaciously to their food habits, especially in the big cities. In Paris wheaten bread, preferably not too dark in color or rough in texture, remained the litmus of minimal well-being. A kind of bread taxis shaped the behavior of many Parisians.[329] They resisted any attempt to divert them from this preoccupation. They regarded ersatz as nothing other than a weapon turned on them by the plotters. It was rejected as demeaning, as nutritionally inadequate at best and as unfit to eat at worst, and, at the extreme, as an insidious effort to undermine their very way of life.

In the aftermath of subsistence crises, the government sometimes took steps which served to confirm many of the gravest suspicions of the famine plot persuasion. For example, in 1726 the duc de Bourbon was dismissed and his mistress and the Pâris brothers were sent into exile. What must the public have made of this? Could it have simply been coincidence that the protagonists of the famine plot were shamefully disgraced in a single blow, many people must have wondered? Turgot's ascension to the ministry had a similar effect. His sweeping, indiscriminate denunciation of all public provisioning operations as inevitably wasteful, fraudulent, and inimical to the public interest was an implicit vindication of Leprévost de Beaumont. Turgot made it seem quite credible that a famine plot or something resembling it operated in earlier times. Finally, as if the government began to believe some of the charges that inspired the famine plot persuasion, in the period following a subsistence crisis it frequently subjected its own provisioning agents to a kind of lynching. It found grave faults in their management, it rejected their accounts as bloated and self-serving, and it subjected them to a quasi-public humiliation. This, too, seemed to confirm the worst suspicions.

Public provisioning was not exclusively an affair of the king and the central government. Representatives of municipalities, organizations of

---

sur le conte du Roy que l'on fait venir des bleds, le ministre n'a qu'à ordonner qu'il ne soient vendu qu'un prix raisonnable [sic]." Gazetins de police, 17 November 1740, MS. Bast. 10167, fol. 175.

[329] See P. Sorokin, *Hunger as a Factor in Human Affairs* (Gainesville, 1975), pp. 88–89.

abundance or public granaries, public assistance institutions, religious communities, the army and navy, and educational institutions competed for surplus grain with royal agents on the domestic and even on the international markets. There was inadequate coordination from above. As a result, there was considerable waste, duplication of effort, and conflict. All these operations raised questions in the minds of observers.

Subsistence, I have argued, was special in every way. But virtually every activity of the government, whether in the subsistence sector or elsewhere, was besmirched by the stigma of fiscality. Whatever the project, it was suspected that somehow it was a ploy or a cover for further exactions. The king's grain may have been perceived as another device meant to raise money for the insatiable royal court and royal administration. The fiscal stereotype was indelibly imprinted in the public mind. It was no accident that Leprévost talked of farms, leases, *partisans, croupiers*—the language of fiscality—when he discussed the details of the famine plot or that Terray was accused of "working grain *en finances.*"[330]

Fiscal maneuvers were ineluctably linked to court capitalism. The power of the financiers and the bankers was greatly feared. Moreover, it was considered illegitimate and dangerous. These money men were frequently parvenus and they were often also foreigners of dubious catholicity. They profited from the nation's miseries and they ensnared kings and ministers in their subtle traps. They appropriated public funds for their own use. It was bad enough that their wealth was ill-gained, but it was scandalous that it was so excessively bloated. They sullied everything they touched and they seemed to be accountable to no one.

Certain scholars may be inclined to view the famine plot persuasion as a form of collective paranoid ideation. According to this argument, the persuasion evinces signs of chronic delusional psychosis. The delusions are logically elaborated in a more or less coherent system but they are compartmentalized or segregated so that they do not result in general personality disorganization. This paranoia is the product of a jarring sense of insecurity—the world is not felt to be safe. In periods of stress people become increasingly rigid in their thinking. They fail to understand the motives that move others, and, in this instance, the government in particular. They misconstrue easily. They perceive their enemies as leagued together in a nefarious plot to do them in. They see the plot in hyperbolic terms.

The ostensibly paranoid elements, however, must not be allowed to obscure the referents that anchor the famine plot persuasion to reality. There *were* companies, speculations, hoarding, monopoly-like practices in trading, highly-placed individuals involved in grain dealings undertaken in the king's name, compromising associations, and so on. Grain was exported when it was in short supply at home. Rotten grain was marketed in some

---

[330] Soulavie, ed., *Mémoires de M. le duc de Choiseul* (Paris, 1790), 1: 42.

places in the king's name. Grain was occasionally thrown into rivers for various reasons. None of these incidents was imaginary. Fears about subsistence were hardly delusional. There was a certain *vraisemblance* in the famine plot persuasion.

Another version of the paranoia argument would link it with the developmental cycle. Since one encounters similar patterns of ideation in certain Third World experiences today, it might be tempting to explain the paranoid discourse expressed in the famine plot persuasion as a function of the underdevelopment of pre- or proto-industrial society. Yet current American attitudes about the oil supply and price situation should serve to remind us that this discourse is no more the exclusive apanage of underdevelopment than are insecurity and stress.

Nor was the eighteenth-century insistence on conspiracy necessarily a psychological distortion. The everyday world of the old regime was replete with plots; the plot vision was not exclusively a stress tropism. Court intrigues and neofeudal clientage systems at the top established a certain conspiratorial model. And conspiracy probably best described the way in which power was used and abused in the village assembly, for example, or the municipal council, the guild, and the church.

The plot thesis was so attractive because there seemed to be no other way to account for the crises. There were plausible reasons for finding the "natural" explanation inadequate. As they looked around them, contemporaries discovered a stunning coherence in *faits divers* which ordinarily would not have yielded any global meaning or commanded general attention. They fitted together like the pieces of a puzzle and they invariably pointed to a plot. How else could a phony dearth have been orchestrated? It required secret and concerted action against the public interest which could only result from conspiracy. Moreover, even if a plot could not be inferred from the events themselves, one could not help discerning a plot once one scrutinized the list of suspects. They were all related, in one sense or another. They represented interlocking loci of power and wealth, a who's who of old regime influence. Fruit of a certain collective mentality, the conspiratorial view was also the source of a kind of heroic countersolidarity. The lines were drawn and the tocsin sounded. The innocence of the consumer-people contrasted vividly with the odiousness of the plotters, who were veritable outlaws. The people-victim found unity and strength in their common predicament—strength for protest and vengeance. Underlying this conspiratorial vision was a naive optimism about the subsistence problem. Things would automatically return to normal once the cabal of bandits was driven from power.

The famine plot persuasion was a vital part of the collective mentality of the old regime. It bespoke the preoccupations and the anguish of proto-industrial, cereal-dependent society. It was not an aberration; rather, given the environment in which it emerged, it was in a sense quite predictable. It required no particular gift for credulity nor a susceptibility to pathology to believe in the famine plot idea in its most rudimentary form. Nor was it merely a fleeting albeit recurrent psychosomatic eruption. It seems to have had a cumulative impact, perhaps even unknown to contemporaries. The famine plot persuasion mobilized large numbers of Frenchmen and helped to politicize them.[331] It accustomed them to perceive subsistence as a political question and to consider it as the measure of a government's commitment to the public interest. Even as the dreadful plot accusations heaped odium on kings, so they prompted the people to question the very meaning of kingship. I would be tempted to suggest that the eighteenth century witnessed a process of mutual disenchantment: the famine plot persuasion undermined popular allegiance to kingship, and the king and government became increasingly convinced that ingratitude was the only sentiment the people knew.[332]

The famine plot persuasion exposed the treason of kingship, the treason by which the king seemed to violate a consensual taboo, to desacralize bread. By this very gesture the famine plot persuasion simultaneously de-sacralized kingship: kingship could no longer command deference and sub-mission in the magical and mystical way it had before. The king and the people released each other from the bonds and obligations that had linked them in a family union. Though it was profoundly subversive, there was nothing revolutionary about the famine persuasion. On the contrary, it affirmed a reactionary attitude, favoring the old moral values of traditional, paternalistic, immobile society.[333] Yet, in the same stroke, by desacralizing bread and kingship, the famine plot persuasion satisfied two of the basic prerequisites for the modernization of the political, psychological, and economic structures of old-regime society.

---

[331] The parlements helped in this process, sometimes despite themselves. See Kaplan, *Bread, Politics and Political Economy.* Of course, subsistence was not the only politicizing issue in the eighteenth-century parlementary discourse.

[332] It would be interesting to try to map out the role of the Enlightenment in this process. The new political economy helped to drive a wedge between the king/government and the people, teaching the former to regard the latter frankly as an obstacle to development. It may also be fruitful to consider the experience of political and moral alienation that touched more and more Frenchmen in the course of the century as part of the larger phenomenon called Enlightenment. But that would require a willingness to rethink more or less radically the meaning of enlightenment and of the Enlightenment. Concretely, for example, it would oblige us to abandon the timeworn, top-to-bottom diffusion model, to renounce the old manichean-isms which merely reify eighteenth-century polemical positions (e.g., classifying the parle-ments and the church monolithically as forces of darkness pitted against the modernizing forces of light represented by the salon-ministerial nexus), and more generally to reintegrate the study of the Enlightenment into the social history of eighteenth-century France. It may be that in some way what we call the Enlightenment drew upon the famine plot persuasion (despite its "benightedness") or helped to channel it in new directions, especially after mid-century. This line of inquiry suggests the need to explore systematically the structural origins of the Enlightenment.

[333] On the "moral" exigencies of subsistence in the English context, see E. P. Thompson, "The Moral Economy of the English Crowd in the Eighteenth Century," *Past and Present*, 52 (February 1971): 76-131. On the moral economy in France, in addition to Kaplan, *Bread, Politics and Political Economy*, see William Reddy, "The Textile Trade and the Language of the Crowd at Rouen, 1752-1871," *Past and Present*, 74 (1977): 62-89 and Louise A. Tilly, "The Food Riot as a Form of Political Conflict in France," *Journal of Interdisciplinary History*, 2 (1971): 23-57.

INDEX

www.ingramcontent.com/pod-product-compliance
Lightning Source LLC
Chambersburg PA
CBHW050926150426
42812CB00051B/2418